Income

Dates _____

Income Source	Budgeted	Amount	Remaining Income	Amount
	$	$	Total Income	$
	$	$	Total Expenses	$
	$	$	Remaining	$
Total	$	$	Total	$

Expenses

Expense	Budgeted	Amount	Expense	Budgeted	Amount
	$	$		$	$
	$	$		$	$
	$	$		$	$
	$	$		$	$
	$	$		$	$
	$	$		$	$
	$	$		$	$
	$	$		$	$
	$	$		$	$
Total	$	$	Total	$	$

Debt Repayment

Creditor	Balance	Paid
	$	$
	$	$
	$	$

Savings

Account	Goal	Amount
	$	$
	$	$

Income

Dates _____

Income Source	Budgeted	Amount	Remaining Income	Amount
	$	$	Total Income	$
	$	$	Total Expenses	$
	$	$	Remaining	$
Total	$	$	Total	$

Expenses

Expense	Budgeted	Amount	Expense	Budgeted	Amount
	$	$		$	$
	$	$		$	$
	$	$		$	$
	$	$		$	$
	$	$		$	$
	$	$		$	$
	$	$		$	$
	$	$		$	$
	$	$		$	$
Total	$	$	Total	$	$

Debt Repayment

Creditor	Balance	Paid
	$	$
	$	$
	$	$

Savings

Account	Goal	Amount
	$	$
	$	$

Income

Dates _____

Income Source	Budgeted	Amount	Remaining Income	Amount
	$	$	Total Income	$
	$	$	Total Expenses	$
	$	$	Remaining	$
Total	$	$	Total	$

Expenses

Expense	Budgeted	Amount	Expense	Budgeted	Amount
	$	$		$	$
	$	$		$	$
	$	$		$	$
	$	$		$	$
	$	$		$	$
	$	$		$	$
	$	$		$	$
	$	$		$	$
	$	$		$	$
Total	$	$	Total	$	$

Debt Repayment

Creditor	Balance	Paid
	$	$
	$	$
	$	$

Savings

Account	Goal	Amount
	$	$
	$	$

Income

Dates _____

Income Source	Budgeted	Amount	Remaining Income	Amount
	$	$	Total Income	$
	$	$	Total Expenses	$
	$	$	Remaining	$
Total	$	$	Total	$

Expenses

Expense	Budgeted	Amount	Expense	Budgeted	Amount
	$	$		$	$
	$	$		$	$
	$	$		$	$
	$	$		$	$
	$	$		$	$
	$	$		$	$
	$	$		$	$
	$	$		$	$
	$	$		$	$
Total	$	$	Total	$	$

Debt Repayment

Creditor	Balance	Paid
	$	$
	$	$
	$	$

Savings

Account	Goal	Amount
	$	$
	$	$

Dates _____

Income

Income Source	Budgeted	Amount	Remaining Income	Amount
	$	$	Total Income	$
	$	$	Total Expenses	$
	$	$	Remaining	$
Total	$	$	Total	$

Expenses

Expense	Budgeted	Amount	Expense	Budgeted	Amount
	$	$		$	$
	$	$		$	$
	$	$		$	$
	$	$		$	$
	$	$		$	$
	$	$		$	$
	$	$		$	$
	$	$		$	$
	$	$		$	$
Total	$	$	Total	$	$

Debt Repayment

Creditor	Balance	Paid
	$	$
	$	$
	$	$

Savings

Account	Goal	Amount
	$	$
	$	$

Income

Dates _____

Income Source	Budgeted	Amount	Remaining Income	Amount
	$	$	Total Income	$
	$	$	Total Expenses	$
	$	$	Remaining	$
Total	$	$	Total	$

Expenses

Expense	Budgeted	Amount	Expense	Budgeted	Amount
	$	$		$	$
	$	$		$	$
	$	$		$	$
	$	$		$	$
	$	$		$	$
	$	$		$	$
	$	$		$	$
	$	$		$	$
	$	$		$	$
Total	$	$	Total	$	$

Debt Repayment

Creditor	Balance	Paid
	$	$
	$	$
	$	$

Savings

Account	Goal	Amount
	$	$
	$	$

Income

Dates _____

Income Source	Budgeted	Amount	Remaining Income	Amount
	$	$	Total Income	$
	$	$	Total Expenses	$
	$	$	Remaining	$
Total	$	$	Total	$

Expenses

Expense	Budgeted	Amount	Expense	Budgeted	Amount
	$	$		$	$
	$	$		$	$
	$	$		$	$
	$	$		$	$
	$	$		$	$
	$	$		$	$
	$	$		$	$
	$	$		$	$
	$	$		$	$
Total	$	$	Total	$	$

Debt Repayment

Creditor	Balance	Paid
	$	$
	$	$
	$	$

Savings

Account	Goal	Amount
	$	$
	$	$

Income

Dates _____

Income Source	Budgeted	Amount	Remaining Income	Amount
	$	$	Total Income	$
	$	$	Total Expenses	$
	$	$	Remaining	$
Total	$	$	Total	$

Expenses

Expense	Budgeted	Amount	Expense	Budgeted	Amount
	$	$		$	$
	$	$		$	$
	$	$		$	$
	$	$		$	$
	$	$		$	$
	$	$		$	$
	$	$		$	$
	$	$		$	$
	$	$		$	$
Total	$	$	Total	$	$

Debt Repayment

Creditor	Balance	Paid
	$	$
	$	$
	$	$

Savings

Account	Goal	Amount
	$	$
	$	$

Income

Dates _____

Income Source	Budgeted	Amount	Remaining Income	Amount
	$	$	Total Income	$
	$	$	Total Expenses	$
	$	$	Remaining	$
Total	$	$	Total	$

Expenses

Expense	Budgeted	Amount	Expense	Budgeted	Amount
	$	$		$	$
	$	$		$	$
	$	$		$	$
	$	$		$	$
	$	$		$	$
	$	$		$	$
	$	$		$	$
	$	$		$	$
	$	$		$	$
Total	$	$	Total	$	$

Debt Repayment

Creditor	Balance	Paid
	$	$
	$	$
	$	$

Savings

Account	Goal	Amount
	$	$
	$	$

Income

Dates _____

Income Source	Budgeted	Amount	Remaining Income	Amount
	$	$	Total Income	$
	$	$	Total Expenses	$
	$	$	Remaining	$
Total	$	$	Total	$

Expenses

Expense	Budgeted	Amount	Expense	Budgeted	Amount
	$	$		$	$
	$	$		$	$
	$	$		$	$
	$	$		$	$
	$	$		$	$
	$	$		$	$
	$	$		$	$
	$	$		$	$
	$	$		$	$
Total	$	$	Total	$	$

Debt Repayment

Creditor	Balance	Paid
	$	$
	$	$
	$	$

Savings

Account	Goal	Amount
	$	$
	$	$

Income

Dates _____

Income Source	Budgeted	Amount	Remaining Income	Amount
	$	$	Total Income	$
	$	$	Total Expenses	$
	$	$	Remaining	$
Total	$	$	Total	$

Expenses

Expense	Budgeted	Amount	Expense	Budgeted	Amount
	$	$		$	$
	$	$		$	$
	$	$		$	$
	$	$		$	$
	$	$		$	$
	$	$		$	$
	$	$		$	$
	$	$		$	$
	$	$		$	$
Total	$	$	Total	$	$

Debt Repayment

Creditor	Balance	Paid
	$	$
	$	$
	$	$

Savings

Account	Goal	Amount
	$	$
	$	$

Income

Dates _____

Income Source	Budgeted	Amount	Remaining Income	Amount
	$	$	Total Income	$
	$	$	Total Expenses	$
	$	$	Remaining	$
Total	$	$	Total	$

Expenses

Expense	Budgeted	Amount	Expense	Budgeted	Amount
	$	$		$	$
	$	$		$	$
	$	$		$	$
	$	$		$	$
	$	$		$	$
	$	$		$	$
	$	$		$	$
	$	$		$	$
	$	$		$	$
Total	$	$	Total	$	$

Debt Repayment

Creditor	Balance	Paid
	$	$
	$	$
	$	$

Savings

Account	Goal	Amount
	$	$
	$	$

Income

Dates _____

Income Source	Budgeted	Amount	Remaining Income	Amount
	$	$	Total Income	$
	$	$	Total Expenses	$
	$	$	Remaining	$
Total	$	$	Total	$

Expenses

Expense	Budgeted	Amount	Expense	Budgeted	Amount
	$	$		$	$
	$	$		$	$
	$	$		$	$
	$	$		$	$
	$	$		$	$
	$	$		$	$
	$	$		$	$
	$	$		$	$
	$	$		$	$
Total	$	$	Total	$	$

Debt Repayment

Creditor	Balance	Paid
	$	$
	$	$
	$	$

Savings

Account	Goal	Amount
	$	$
	$	$

Income

Dates _____

Income Source	Budgeted	Amount	Remaining Income	Amount
	$	$	Total Income	$
	$	$	Total Expenses	$
	$	$	Remaining	$
Total	$	$	Total	$

Expenses

Expense	Budgeted	Amount	Expense	Budgeted	Amount
	$	$		$	$
	$	$		$	$
	$	$		$	$
	$	$		$	$
	$	$		$	$
	$	$		$	$
	$	$		$	$
	$	$		$	$
	$	$		$	$
Total	$	$	Total	$	$

Debt Repayment

Creditor	Balance	Paid
	$	$
	$	$
	$	$

Savings

Account	Goal	Amount
	$	$
	$	$

Income

Dates _____

Income Source	Budgeted	Amount	Remaining Income	Amount
	$	$	Total Income	$
	$	$	Total Expenses	$
	$	$	Remaining	$
Total	$	$	Total	$

Expenses

Expense	Budgeted	Amount	Expense	Budgeted	Amount
	$	$		$	$
	$	$		$	$
	$	$		$	$
	$	$		$	$
	$	$		$	$
	$	$		$	$
	$	$		$	$
	$	$		$	$
	$	$		$	$
Total	$	$	Total	$	$

Debt Repayment

Creditor	Balance	Paid
	$	$
	$	$
	$	$

Savings

Account	Goal	Amount
	$	$
	$	$

Income

Dates _____

Income Source	Budgeted	Amount	Remaining Income	Amount
	$	$	Total Income	$
	$	$	Total Expenses	$
	$	$	Remaining	$
Total	$	$	Total	$

Expenses

Expense	Budgeted	Amount	Expense	Budgeted	Amount
	$	$		$	$
	$	$		$	$
	$	$		$	$
	$	$		$	$
	$	$		$	$
	$	$		$	$
	$	$		$	$
	$	$		$	$
	$	$		$	$
Total	$	$	Total	$	$

Debt Repayment

Creditor	Balance	Paid
	$	$
	$	$
	$	$

Savings

Account	Goal	Amount
	$	$
	$	$

Income

Dates _____

Income Source	Budgeted	Amount	Remaining Income	Amount
	$	$	Total Income	$
	$	$	Total Expenses	$
	$	$	Remaining	$
Total	$	$	Total	$

Expenses

Expense	Budgeted	Amount	Expense	Budgeted	Amount
	$	$		$	$
	$	$		$	$
	$	$		$	$
	$	$		$	$
	$	$		$	$
	$	$		$	$
	$	$		$	$
	$	$		$	$
	$	$		$	$
Total	$	$	Total	$	$

Debt Repayment

Creditor	Balance	Paid
	$	$
	$	$
	$	$

Savings

Account	Goal	Amount
	$	$
	$	$

Income

Dates _____

Income Source	Budgeted	Amount	Remaining Income	Amount
	$	$	Total Income	$
	$	$	Total Expenses	$
	$	$	Remaining	$
Total	$	$	Total	$

Expenses

Expense	Budgeted	Amount	Expense	Budgeted	Amount
	$	$		$	$
	$	$		$	$
	$	$		$	$
	$	$		$	$
	$	$		$	$
	$	$		$	$
	$	$		$	$
	$	$		$	$
	$	$		$	$
Total	$	$	Total	$	$

Debt Repayment

Creditor	Balance	Paid
	$	$
	$	$
	$	$

Savings

Account	Goal	Amount
	$	$
	$	$

Dates _____

Income

Income Source	Budgeted	Amount	Remaining Income	Amount
	$	$	Total Income	$
	$	$	Total Expenses	$
	$	$	Remaining	$
Total	$	$	Total	$

Expenses

Expense	Budgeted	Amount	Expense	Budgeted	Amount
	$	$		$	$
	$	$		$	$
	$	$		$	$
	$	$		$	$
	$	$		$	$
	$	$		$	$
	$	$		$	$
	$	$		$	$
	$	$		$	$
Total	$	$	Total	$	$

Debt Repayment

Creditor	Balance	Paid
	$	$
	$	$
	$	$

Savings

Account	Goal	Amount
	$	$
	$	$

Income

Dates _____

Income Source	Budgeted	Amount	Remaining Income	Amount
	$	$	Total Income	$
	$	$	Total Expenses	$
	$	$	Remaining	$
Total	$	$	Total	$

Expenses

Expense	Budgeted	Amount	Expense	Budgeted	Amount
	$	$		$	$
	$	$		$	$
	$	$		$	$
	$	$		$	$
	$	$		$	$
	$	$		$	$
	$	$		$	$
	$	$		$	$
	$	$		$	$
Total	$	$	Total	$	$

Debt Repayment

Creditor	Balance	Paid
	$	$
	$	$
	$	$

Savings

Account	Goal	Amount
	$	$
	$	$

Income

Dates _____

Income Source	Budgeted	Amount	Remaining Income	Amount
	$	$	Total Income	$
	$	$	Total Expenses	$
	$	$	Remaining	$
Total	$	$	Total	$

Expenses

Expense	Budgeted	Amount	Expense	Budgeted	Amount
	$	$		$	$
	$	$		$	$
	$	$		$	$
	$	$		$	$
	$	$		$	$
	$	$		$	$
	$	$		$	$
	$	$		$	$
	$	$		$	$
Total	$	$	Total	$	$

Debt Repayment

Creditor	Balance	Paid
	$	$
	$	$
	$	$

Savings

Account	Goal	Amount
	$	$
	$	$

Income

Dates _____

Income Source	Budgeted	Amount	Remaining Income	Amount
	$	$	Total Income	$
	$	$	Total Expenses	$
	$	$	Remaining	$
Total	$	$	Total	$

Expenses

Expense	Budgeted	Amount	Expense	Budgeted	Amount
	$	$		$	$
	$	$		$	$
	$	$		$	$
	$	$		$	$
	$	$		$	$
	$	$		$	$
	$	$		$	$
	$	$		$	$
	$	$		$	$
Total	$	$	Total	$	$

Debt Repayment

Creditor	Balance	Paid
	$	$
	$	$
	$	$

Savings

Account	Goal	Amount
	$	$
	$	$

Income

Dates _____

Income Source	Budgeted	Amount	Remaining Income	Amount
	$	$	Total Income	$
	$	$	Total Expenses	$
	$	$	Remaining	$
Total	$	$	Total	$

Expenses

Expense	Budgeted	Amount	Expense	Budgeted	Amount
	$	$		$	$
	$	$		$	$
	$	$		$	$
	$	$		$	$
	$	$		$	$
	$	$		$	$
	$	$		$	$
	$	$		$	$
	$	$		$	$
Total	$	$	Total	$	$

Debt Repayment

Creditor	Balance	Paid
	$	$
	$	$
	$	$

Savings

Account	Goal	Amount
	$	$
	$	$

Income

Dates _____

Income Source	Budgeted	Amount	Remaining Income	Amount
	$	$	Total Income	$
	$	$	Total Expenses	$
	$	$	Remaining	$
Total	$	$	Total	$

Expenses

Expense	Budgeted	Amount	Expense	Budgeted	Amount
	$	$		$	$
	$	$		$	$
	$	$		$	$
	$	$		$	$
	$	$		$	$
	$	$		$	$
	$	$		$	$
	$	$		$	$
	$	$		$	$
Total	$	$	Total	$	$

Debt Repayment

Creditor	Balance	Paid
	$	$
	$	$
	$	$

Savings

Account	Goal	Amount
	$	$
	$	$

Dates _____

Income

Income Source	Budgeted	Amount	Remaining Income	Amount
	$	$	Total Income	$
	$	$	Total Expenses	$
	$	$	Remaining	$
Total	$	$	Total	$

Expenses

Expense	Budgeted	Amount	Expense	Budgeted	Amount
	$	$		$	$
	$	$		$	$
	$	$		$	$
	$	$		$	$
	$	$		$	$
	$	$		$	$
	$	$		$	$
	$	$		$	$
	$	$		$	$
Total	$	$	Total	$	$

Debt Repayment

Creditor	Balance	Paid
	$	$
	$	$
	$	$

Savings

Account	Goal	Amount
	$	$
	$	$

Income

Dates _____

Income Source	Budgeted	Amount	Remaining Income	Amount
	$	$	Total Income	$
	$	$	Total Expenses	$
	$	$	Remaining	$
Total	$	$	Total	$

Expenses

Expense	Budgeted	Amount	Expense	Budgeted	Amount
	$	$		$	$
	$	$		$	$
	$	$		$	$
	$	$		$	$
	$	$		$	$
	$	$		$	$
	$	$		$	$
	$	$		$	$
	$	$		$	$
Total	$	$	Total	$	$

Debt Repayment

Creditor	Balance	Paid
	$	$
	$	$
	$	$

Savings

Account	Goal	Amount
	$	$
	$	$

Income

Dates _____

Income Source	Budgeted	Amount	Remaining Income	Amount
	$	$	Total Income	$
	$	$	Total Expenses	$
	$	$	Remaining	$
Total	$	$	Total	$

Expenses

Expense	Budgeted	Amount	Expense	Budgeted	Amount
	$	$		$	$
	$	$		$	$
	$	$		$	$
	$	$		$	$
	$	$		$	$
	$	$		$	$
	$	$		$	$
	$	$		$	$
Total	$	$	Total	$	$

Debt Repayment

Creditor	Balance	Paid
	$	$
	$	$
	$	$

Savings

Account	Goal	Amount
	$	$
	$	$

Income

Dates _____

Income Source	Budgeted	Amount	Remaining Income	Amount
	$	$	Total Income	$
	$	$	Total Expenses	$
	$	$	Remaining	$
Total	$	$	Total	$

Expenses

Expense	Budgeted	Amount	Expense	Budgeted	Amount
	$	$		$	$
	$	$		$	$
	$	$		$	$
	$	$		$	$
	$	$		$	$
	$	$		$	$
	$	$		$	$
	$	$		$	$
	$	$		$	$
Total	$	$	Total	$	$

Debt Repayment

Creditor	Balance	Paid
	$	$
	$	$
	$	$

Savings

Account	Goal	Amount
	$	$
	$	$

Income

Dates _____

Income Source	Budgeted	Amount	Remaining Income	Amount
	$	$	Total Income	$
	$	$	Total Expenses	$
	$	$	Remaining	$
Total	$	$	Total	$

Expenses

Expense	Budgeted	Amount	Expense	Budgeted	Amount
	$	$		$	$
	$	$		$	$
	$	$		$	$
	$	$		$	$
	$	$		$	$
	$	$		$	$
	$	$		$	$
	$	$		$	$
	$	$		$	$
Total	$	$	Total	$	$

Debt Repayment

Creditor	Balance	Paid
	$	$
	$	$
	$	$

Savings

Account	Goal	Amount
	$	$
	$	$

Income

Dates _____

Income Source	Budgeted	Amount	Remaining Income	Amount
	$	$	Total Income	$
	$	$	Total Expenses	$
	$	$	Remaining	$
Total	$	$	Total	$

Expenses

Expense	Budgeted	Amount	Expense	Budgeted	Amount
	$	$		$	$
	$	$		$	$
	$	$		$	$
	$	$		$	$
	$	$		$	$
	$	$		$	$
	$	$		$	$
	$	$		$	$
	$	$		$	$
Total	$	$	Total	$	$

Debt Repayment

Creditor			Balance	Paid
			$	$
			$	$
			$	$

Savings

Account			Goal	Amount
			$	$
			$	$

Income

Dates _____

Income Source	Budgeted	Amount	Remaining Income	Amount
	$	$	Total Income	$
	$	$	Total Expenses	$
	$	$	Remaining	$
Total	$	$	Total	$

Expenses

Expense	Budgeted	Amount	Expense	Budgeted	Amount
	$	$		$	$
	$	$		$	$
	$	$		$	$
	$	$		$	$
	$	$		$	$
	$	$		$	$
	$	$		$	$
	$	$		$	$
	$	$		$	$
Total	$	$	Total	$	$

Debt Repayment

Creditor	Balance	Paid
	$	$
	$	$
	$	$

Savings

Account	Goal	Amount
	$	$
	$	$

Income

Dates _____

Income Source	Budgeted	Amount	Remaining Income	Amount
	$	$	Total Income	$
	$	$	Total Expenses	$
	$	$	Remaining	$
Total	$	$	Total	$

Expenses

Expense	Budgeted	Amount	Expense	Budgeted	Amount
	$	$		$	$
	$	$		$	$
	$	$		$	$
	$	$		$	$
	$	$		$	$
	$	$		$	$
	$	$		$	$
	$	$		$	$
	$	$		$	$
Total	$	$	Total	$	$

Debt Repayment

Creditor	Balance	Paid
	$	$
	$	$
	$	$

Savings

Account	Goal	Amount
	$	$
	$	$

Income

Dates _____

Income Source	Budgeted	Amount	Remaining Income	Amount
	$	$	Total Income	$
	$	$	Total Expenses	$
	$	$	Remaining	$
Total	$	$	Total	$

Expenses

Expense	Budgeted	Amount	Expense	Budgeted	Amount
	$	$		$	$
	$	$		$	$
	$	$		$	$
	$	$		$	$
	$	$		$	$
	$	$		$	$
	$	$		$	$
	$	$		$	$
	$	$		$	$
Total	$	$	Total	$	$

Debt Repayment

Creditor	Balance	Paid
	$	$
	$	$
	$	$

Savings

Account	Goal	Amount
	$	$
	$	$

Income

Dates _____

Income Source	Budgeted	Amount	Remaining Income	Amount
	$	$	Total Income	$
	$	$	Total Expenses	$
	$	$	Remaining	$
Total	$	$	Total	$

Expenses

Expense	Budgeted	Amount	Expense	Budgeted	Amount
	$	$		$	$
	$	$		$	$
	$	$		$	$
	$	$		$	$
	$	$		$	$
	$	$		$	$
	$	$		$	$
	$	$		$	$
	$	$		$	$
Total	$	$	Total	$	$

Debt Repayment

Creditor	Balance	Paid
	$	$
	$	$
	$	$

Savings

Account	Goal	Amount
	$	$
	$	$

Income

Dates _____

Income Source	Budgeted	Amount	Remaining Income	Amount
	$	$	Total Income	$
	$	$	Total Expenses	$
	$	$	Remaining	$
Total	$	$	Total	$

Expenses

Expense	Budgeted	Amount	Expense	Budgeted	Amount
	$	$		$	$
	$	$		$	$
	$	$		$	$
	$	$		$	$
	$	$		$	$
	$	$		$	$
	$	$		$	$
	$	$		$	$
	$	$		$	$
Total	$	$	Total	$	$

Debt Repayment

Creditor	Balance	Paid
	$	$
	$	$
	$	$

Savings

Account	Goal	Amount
	$	$
	$	$

Income

Dates _____

Income Source	Budgeted	Amount	Remaining Income	Amount
	$	$	Total Income	$
	$	$	Total Expenses	$
	$	$	Remaining	$
Total	$	$	Total	$

Expenses

Expense	Budgeted	Amount	Expense	Budgeted	Amount
	$	$		$	$
	$	$		$	$
	$	$		$	$
	$	$		$	$
	$	$		$	$
	$	$		$	$
	$	$		$	$
	$	$		$	$
	$	$		$	$
Total	$	$	Total	$	$

Debt Repayment

Creditor	Balance	Paid
	$	$
	$	$
	$	$

Savings

Account	Goal	Amount
	$	$
	$	$

Income

Dates _____

Income Source	Budgeted	Amount	Remaining Income	Amount
	$	$	Total Income	$
	$	$	Total Expenses	$
	$	$	Remaining	$
Total	$	$	Total	$

Expenses

Expense	Budgeted	Amount	Expense	Budgeted	Amount
	$	$		$	$
	$	$		$	$
	$	$		$	$
	$	$		$	$
	$	$		$	$
	$	$		$	$
	$	$		$	$
	$	$		$	$
	$	$		$	$
Total	$	$	Total	$	$

Debt Repayment

Creditor	Balance	Paid
	$	$
	$	$
	$	$

Savings

Account	Goal	Amount
	$	$
	$	$

Income

Dates _____

Income Source	Budgeted	Amount	Remaining Income	Amount
	$	$	Total Income	$
	$	$	Total Expenses	$
	$	$	Remaining	$
Total	$	$	Total	$

Expenses

Expense	Budgeted	Amount	Expense	Budgeted	Amount
	$	$		$	$
	$	$		$	$
	$	$		$	$
	$	$		$	$
	$	$		$	$
	$	$		$	$
	$	$		$	$
	$	$		$	$
	$	$		$	$
Total	$	$	Total	$	$

Debt Repayment

Creditor	Balance	Paid
	$	$
	$	$
	$	$

Savings

Account	Goal	Amount
	$	$
	$	$

Income

Dates _____

Income Source	Budgeted	Amount	Remaining Income	Amount
	$	$	Total Income	$
	$	$	Total Expenses	$
	$	$	Remaining	$
Total	$	$	Total	$

Expenses

Expense	Budgeted	Amount	Expense	Budgeted	Amount
	$	$		$	$
	$	$		$	$
	$	$		$	$
	$	$		$	$
	$	$		$	$
	$	$		$	$
	$	$		$	$
	$	$		$	$
	$	$		$	$
Total	$	$	Total	$	$

Debt Repayment

Creditor	Balance	Paid
	$	$
	$	$
	$	$

Savings

Account	Goal	Amount
	$	$
	$	$

Income

Dates _____

Income Source	Budgeted	Amount	Remaining Income	Amount
	$	$	Total Income	$
	$	$	Total Expenses	$
	$	$	Remaining	$
Total	$	$	Total	$

Expenses

Expense	Budgeted	Amount	Expense	Budgeted	Amount
	$	$		$	$
	$	$		$	$
	$	$		$	$
	$	$		$	$
	$	$		$	$
	$	$		$	$
	$	$		$	$
	$	$		$	$
	$	$		$	$
Total	$	$	Total	$	$

Debt Repayment

Creditor	Balance	Paid
	$	$
	$	$
	$	$

Savings

Account	Goal	Amount
	$	$
	$	$

Income

Dates _____

Income Source	Budgeted	Amount	Remaining Income	Amount
	$	$	Total Income	$
	$	$	Total Expenses	$
	$	$	Remaining	$
Total	$	$	Total	$

Expenses

Expense	Budgeted	Amount	Expense	Budgeted	Amount
	$	$		$	$
	$	$		$	$
	$	$		$	$
	$	$		$	$
	$	$		$	$
	$	$		$	$
	$	$		$	$
	$	$		$	$
	$	$		$	$
Total	$	$	Total	$	$

Debt Repayment

Creditor	Balance	Paid
	$	$
	$	$
	$	$

Savings

Account	Goal	Amount
	$	$
	$	$

Income

Dates _____

Income Source	Budgeted	Amount	Remaining Income	Amount
	$	$	Total Income	$
	$	$	Total Expenses	$
	$	$	Remaining	$
Total	$	$	Total	$

Expenses

Expense	Budgeted	Amount	Expense	Budgeted	Amount
	$	$		$	$
	$	$		$	$
	$	$		$	$
	$	$		$	$
	$	$		$	$
	$	$		$	$
	$	$		$	$
	$	$		$	$
	$	$		$	$
Total	$	$	Total	$	$

Debt Repayment

Creditor	Balance	Paid
	$	$
	$	$
	$	$

Savings

Account	Goal	Amount
	$	$
	$	$

Income

Dates _____

Income Source	Budgeted	Amount	Remaining Income	Amount
	$	$	Total Income	$
	$	$	Total Expenses	$
	$	$	Remaining	$
Total	$	$	Total	$

Expenses

Expense	Budgeted	Amount	Expense	Budgeted	Amount
	$	$		$	$
	$	$		$	$
	$	$		$	$
	$	$		$	$
	$	$		$	$
	$	$		$	$
	$	$		$	$
	$	$		$	$
	$	$		$	$
Total	$	$	Total	$	$

Debt Repayment

Creditor	Balance	Paid
	$	$
	$	$
	$	$

Savings

Account	Goal	Amount
	$	$
	$	$

Income

Dates _____

Income Source	Budgeted	Amount	Remaining Income	Amount
	$	$	Total Income	$
	$	$	Total Expenses	$
	$	$	Remaining	$
Total	$	$	Total	$

Expenses

Expense	Budgeted	Amount	Expense	Budgeted	Amount
	$	$		$	$
	$	$		$	$
	$	$		$	$
	$	$		$	$
	$	$		$	$
	$	$		$	$
	$	$		$	$
	$	$		$	$
	$	$		$	$
Total	$	$	Total	$	$

Debt Repayment

Creditor	Balance	Paid
	$	$
	$	$
	$	$

Savings

Account	Goal	Amount
	$	$
	$	$

Income

Dates _____

Income Source	Budgeted	Amount	Remaining Income	Amount
	$	$	Total Income	$
	$	$	Total Expenses	$
	$	$	Remaining	$
Total	$	$	Total	$

Expenses

Expense	Budgeted	Amount	Expense	Budgeted	Amount
	$	$		$	$
	$	$		$	$
	$	$		$	$
	$	$		$	$
	$	$		$	$
	$	$		$	$
	$	$		$	$
	$	$		$	$
	$	$		$	$
Total	$	$	Total	$	$

Debt Repayment

Creditor	Balance	Paid
	$	$
	$	$
	$	$

Savings

Account	Goal	Amount
	$	$
	$	$

Income

Dates _____

Income Source	Budgeted	Amount	Remaining Income	Amount
	$	$	Total Income	$
	$	$	Total Expenses	$
	$	$	Remaining	$
Total	$	$	Total	$

Expenses

Expense	Budgeted	Amount	Expense	Budgeted	Amount
	$	$		$	$
	$	$		$	$
	$	$		$	$
	$	$		$	$
	$	$		$	$
	$	$		$	$
	$	$		$	$
	$	$		$	$
	$	$		$	$
Total	$	$	Total	$	$

Debt Repayment

Creditor	Balance	Paid
	$	$
	$	$
	$	$

Savings

Account	Goal	Amount
	$	$
	$	$

Income

Dates _____

Income Source	Budgeted	Amount	Remaining Income	Amount
	$	$	Total Income	$
	$	$	Total Expenses	$
	$	$	Remaining	$
Total	$	$	Total	$

Expenses

Expense	Budgeted	Amount	Expense	Budgeted	Amount
	$	$		$	$
	$	$		$	$
	$	$		$	$
	$	$		$	$
	$	$		$	$
	$	$		$	$
	$	$		$	$
	$	$		$	$
	$	$		$	$
Total	$	$	Total	$	$

Debt Repayment

Creditor	Balance	Paid
	$	$
	$	$
	$	$

Savings

Account	Goal	Amount
	$	$
	$	$

Income

Dates _____

Income Source	Budgeted	Amount	Remaining Income	Amount
	$	$	Total Income	$
	$	$	Total Expenses	$
	$	$	Remaining	$
Total	$	$	Total	$

Expenses

Expense	Budgeted	Amount	Expense	Budgeted	Amount
	$	$		$	$
	$	$		$	$
	$	$		$	$
	$	$		$	$
	$	$		$	$
	$	$		$	$
	$	$		$	$
	$	$		$	$
	$	$		$	$
Total	$	$	Total	$	$

Debt Repayment

Creditor	Balance	Paid
	$	$
	$	$
	$	$

Savings

Account	Goal	Amount
	$	$
	$	$

Income

Dates _____

Income Source	Budgeted	Amount	Remaining Income	Amount
	$	$	Total Income	$
	$	$	Total Expenses	$
	$	$	Remaining	$
Total	$	$	Total	$

Expenses

Expense	Budgeted	Amount	Expense	Budgeted	Amount
	$	$		$	$
	$	$		$	$
	$	$		$	$
	$	$		$	$
	$	$		$	$
	$	$		$	$
	$	$		$	$
	$	$		$	$
	$	$		$	$
Total	$	$	Total	$	$

Debt Repayment

Creditor	Balance	Paid
	$	$
	$	$
	$	$

Savings

Account	Goal	Amount
	$	$
	$	$

Income

Dates _____

Income Source	Budgeted	Amount	Remaining Income	Amount
	$	$	Total Income	$
	$	$	Total Expenses	$
	$	$	Remaining	$
Total	$	$	Total	$

Expenses

Expense	Budgeted	Amount	Expense	Budgeted	Amount
	$	$		$	$
	$	$		$	$
	$	$		$	$
	$	$		$	$
	$	$		$	$
	$	$		$	$
	$	$		$	$
	$	$		$	$
	$	$		$	$
Total	$	$	Total	$	$

Debt Repayment

Creditor	Balance	Paid
	$	$
	$	$
	$	$

Savings

Account	Goal	Amount
	$	$
	$	$

Income

Dates _____

Income Source	Budgeted	Amount	Remaining Income	Amount
	$	$	Total Income	$
	$	$	Total Expenses	$
	$	$	Remaining	$
Total	$	$	Total	$

Expenses

Expense	Budgeted	Amount	Expense	Budgeted	Amount
	$	$		$	$
	$	$		$	$
	$	$		$	$
	$	$		$	$
	$	$		$	$
	$	$		$	$
	$	$		$	$
	$	$		$	$
	$	$		$	$
Total	$	$	Total	$	$

Debt Repayment

Creditor	Balance	Paid
	$	$
	$	$
	$	$

Savings

Account	Goal	Amount
	$	$
	$	$

Income

Dates _____

Income Source	Budgeted	Amount	Remaining Income	Amount
	$	$	Total Income	$
	$	$	Total Expenses	$
	$	$	Remaining	$
Total	$	$	Total	$

Expenses

Expense	Budgeted	Amount	Expense	Budgeted	Amount
	$	$		$	$
	$	$		$	$
	$	$		$	$
	$	$		$	$
	$	$		$	$
	$	$		$	$
	$	$		$	$
	$	$		$	$
	$	$		$	$
Total	$	$	Total	$	$

Debt Repayment

Creditor	Balance	Paid
	$	$
	$	$
	$	$

Savings

Account	Goal	Amount
	$	$
	$	$

Income

Dates _____

Income Source	Budgeted	Amount	Remaining Income	Amount
	$	$	Total Income	$
	$	$	Total Expenses	$
	$	$	Remaining	$
Total	$	$	Total	$

Expenses

Expense	Budgeted	Amount	Expense	Budgeted	Amount
	$	$		$	$
	$	$		$	$
	$	$		$	$
	$	$		$	$
	$	$		$	$
	$	$		$	$
	$	$		$	$
	$	$		$	$
	$	$		$	$
Total	$	$	Total	$	$

Debt Repayment

Creditor	Balance	Paid
	$	$
	$	$
	$	$

Savings

Account	Goal	Amount
	$	$
	$	$

Income

Dates _____

Income Source	Budgeted	Amount	Remaining Income	Amount
	$	$	Total Income	$
	$	$	Total Expenses	$
	$	$	Remaining	$
Total	$	$	Total	$

Expenses

Expense	Budgeted	Amount	Expense	Budgeted	Amount
	$	$		$	$
	$	$		$	$
	$	$		$	$
	$	$		$	$
	$	$		$	$
	$	$		$	$
	$	$		$	$
	$	$		$	$
	$	$		$	$
Total	$	$	Total	$	$

Debt Repayment

Creditor	Balance	Paid
	$	$
	$	$
	$	$

Savings

Account	Goal	Amount
	$	$
	$	$

Income

Dates _____

Income Source	Budgeted	Amount	Remaining Income	Amount
	$	$	Total Income	$
	$	$	Total Expenses	$
	$	$	Remaining	$
Total	$	$	Total	$

Expenses

Expense	Budgeted	Amount	Expense	Budgeted	Amount
	$	$		$	$
	$	$		$	$
	$	$		$	$
	$	$		$	$
	$	$		$	$
	$	$		$	$
	$	$		$	$
	$	$		$	$
	$	$		$	$
Total	$	$	Total	$	$

Debt Repayment

Creditor	Balance	Paid
	$	$
	$	$
	$	$

Savings

Account	Goal	Amount
	$	$
	$	$

Income

Dates _____

Income Source	Budgeted	Amount	Remaining Income	Amount
	$	$	Total Income	$
	$	$	Total Expenses	$
	$	$	Remaining	$
Total	$	$	Total	$

Expenses

Expense	Budgeted	Amount	Expense	Budgeted	Amount
	$	$		$	$
	$	$		$	$
	$	$		$	$
	$	$		$	$
	$	$		$	$
	$	$		$	$
	$	$		$	$
	$	$		$	$
	$	$		$	$
Total	$	$	Total	$	$

Debt Repayment

Creditor	Balance	Paid
	$	$
	$	$
	$	$

Savings

Account	Goal	Amount
	$	$
	$	$

Income

Dates _____

Income Source	Budgeted	Amount	Remaining Income	Amount
	$	$	Total Income	$
	$	$	Total Expenses	$
	$	$	Remaining	$
Total	$	$	Total	$

Expenses

Expense	Budgeted	Amount	Expense	Budgeted	Amount
	$	$		$	$
	$	$		$	$
	$	$		$	$
	$	$		$	$
	$	$		$	$
	$	$		$	$
	$	$		$	$
	$	$		$	$
	$	$		$	$
Total	$	$	Total	$	$

Debt Repayment

Creditor	Balance	Paid
	$	$
	$	$
	$	$

Savings

Account	Goal	Amount
	$	$
	$	$

Income

Dates _____

Income Source	Budgeted	Amount	Remaining Income	Amount
	$	$	Total Income	$
	$	$	Total Expenses	$
	$	$	Remaining	$
Total	$	$	Total	$

Expenses

Expense	Budgeted	Amount	Expense	Budgeted	Amount
	$	$		$	$
	$	$		$	$
	$	$		$	$
	$	$		$	$
	$	$		$	$
	$	$		$	$
	$	$		$	$
	$	$		$	$
	$	$		$	$
Total	$	$	Total	$	$

Debt Repayment

Creditor	Balance	Paid
	$	$
	$	$
	$	$

Savings

Account	Goal	Amount
	$	$
	$	$

Income

Dates _____

Income Source	Budgeted	Amount	Remaining Income	Amount
	$	$	Total Income	$
	$	$	Total Expenses	$
	$	$	Remaining	$
Total	$	$	Total	$

Expenses

Expense	Budgeted	Amount	Expense	Budgeted	Amount
	$	$		$	$
	$	$		$	$
	$	$		$	$
	$	$		$	$
	$	$		$	$
	$	$		$	$
	$	$		$	$
	$	$		$	$
	$	$		$	$
Total	$	$	Total	$	$

Debt Repayment

Creditor	Balance	Paid
	$	$
	$	$
	$	$

Savings

Account	Goal	Amount
	$	$
	$	$

Income

Dates _____

Income Source	Budgeted	Amount	Remaining Income	Amount
	$	$	Total Income	$
	$	$	Total Expenses	$
	$	$	Remaining	$
Total	$	$	Total	$

Expenses

Expense	Budgeted	Amount	Expense	Budgeted	Amount
	$	$		$	$
	$	$		$	$
	$	$		$	$
	$	$		$	$
	$	$		$	$
	$	$		$	$
	$	$		$	$
	$	$		$	$
	$	$		$	$
Total	$	$	Total	$	$

Debt Repayment

Creditor	Balance	Paid
	$	$
	$	$
	$	$

Savings

Account	Goal	Amount
	$	$
	$	$

Income

Dates _____

Income Source	Budgeted	Amount	Remaining Income	Amount
	$	$	Total Income	$
	$	$	Total Expenses	$
	$	$	Remaining	$
Total	$	$	Total	$

Expenses

Expense	Budgeted	Amount	Expense	Budgeted	Amount
	$	$		$	$
	$	$		$	$
	$	$		$	$
	$	$		$	$
	$	$		$	$
	$	$		$	$
	$	$		$	$
	$	$		$	$
	$	$		$	$
Total	$	$	Total	$	$

Debt Repayment

Creditor	Balance	Paid
	$	$
	$	$
	$	$

Savings

Account	Goal	Amount
	$	$
	$	$

Income

Dates _____

Income Source	Budgeted	Amount	Remaining Income	Amount
	$	$	Total Income	$
	$	$	Total Expenses	$
	$	$	Remaining	$
Total	$	$	Total	$

Expenses

Expense	Budgeted	Amount	Expense	Budgeted	Amount
	$	$		$	$
	$	$		$	$
	$	$		$	$
	$	$		$	$
	$	$		$	$
	$	$		$	$
	$	$		$	$
	$	$		$	$
	$	$		$	$
Total	$	$	Total	$	$

Debt Repayment

Creditor	Balance	Paid
	$	$
	$	$
	$	$

Savings

Account	Goal	Amount
	$	$
	$	$

Income

Dates _____

Income Source	Budgeted	Amount	Remaining Income	Amount
	$	$	Total Income	$
	$	$	Total Expenses	$
	$	$	Remaining	$
Total	$	$	Total	$

Expenses

Expense	Budgeted	Amount	Expense	Budgeted	Amount
	$	$		$	$
	$	$		$	$
	$	$		$	$
	$	$		$	$
	$	$		$	$
	$	$		$	$
	$	$		$	$
	$	$		$	$
	$	$		$	$
Total	$	$	Total	$	$

Debt Repayment

Creditor	Balance	Paid
	$	$
	$	$
	$	$

Savings

Account	Goal	Amount
	$	$
	$	$

Income

Dates _____

Income Source	Budgeted	Amount	Remaining Income	Amount
	$	$	Total Income	$
	$	$	Total Expenses	$
	$	$	Remaining	$
Total	$	$	Total	$

Expenses

Expense	Budgeted	Amount	Expense	Budgeted	Amount
	$	$		$	$
	$	$		$	$
	$	$		$	$
	$	$		$	$
	$	$		$	$
	$	$		$	$
	$	$		$	$
	$	$		$	$
	$	$		$	$
Total	$	$	Total	$	$

Debt Repayment

Creditor	Balance	Paid
	$	$
	$	$
	$	$

Savings

Account	Goal	Amount
	$	$
	$	$

Income

Dates _____

Income Source	Budgeted	Amount	Remaining Income	Amount
	$	$	Total Income	$
	$	$	Total Expenses	$
	$	$	Remaining	$
Total	$	$	Total	$

Expenses

Expense	Budgeted	Amount	Expense	Budgeted	Amount
	$	$		$	$
	$	$		$	$
	$	$		$	$
	$	$		$	$
	$	$		$	$
	$	$		$	$
	$	$		$	$
	$	$		$	$
	$	$		$	$
Total	$	$	Total	$	$

Debt Repayment

Creditor	Balance	Paid
	$	$
	$	$
	$	$

Savings

Account	Goal	Amount
	$	$
	$	$

Income

Dates _____

Income Source	Budgeted	Amount	Remaining Income	Amount
	$	$	Total Income	$
	$	$	Total Expenses	$
	$	$	Remaining	$
Total	$	$	Total	$

Expenses

Expense	Budgeted	Amount	Expense	Budgeted	Amount
	$	$		$	$
	$	$		$	$
	$	$		$	$
	$	$		$	$
	$	$		$	$
	$	$		$	$
	$	$		$	$
	$	$		$	$
	$	$		$	$
Total	$	$	Total	$	$

Debt Repayment

Creditor	Balance	Paid
	$	$
	$	$
	$	$

Savings

Account	Goal	Amount
	$	$
	$	$

Income

Dates _____

Income Source	Budgeted	Amount	Remaining Income	Amount
	$	$	Total Income	$
	$	$	Total Expenses	$
	$	$	Remaining	$
Total	$	$	Total	$

Expenses

Expense	Budgeted	Amount	Expense	Budgeted	Amount
	$	$		$	$
	$	$		$	$
	$	$		$	$
	$	$		$	$
	$	$		$	$
	$	$		$	$
	$	$		$	$
	$	$		$	$
	$	$		$	$
Total	$	$	Total	$	$

Debt Repayment

Creditor	Balance	Paid
	$	$
	$	$
	$	$

Savings

Account	Goal	Amount
	$	$
	$	$

Income

Dates _____

Income Source	Budgeted	Amount	Remaining Income	Amount
	$	$	Total Income	$
	$	$	Total Expenses	$
	$	$	Remaining	$
Total	$	$	Total	$

Expenses

Expense	Budgeted	Amount	Expense	Budgeted	Amount
	$	$		$	$
	$	$		$	$
	$	$		$	$
	$	$		$	$
	$	$		$	$
	$	$		$	$
	$	$		$	$
	$	$		$	$
	$	$		$	$
Total	$	$	Total	$	$

Debt Repayment

Creditor	Balance	Paid
	$	$
	$	$
	$	$

Savings

Account	Goal	Amount
	$	$
	$	$

Income

Dates _____

Income Source	Budgeted	Amount	Remaining Income	Amount
	$	$	Total Income	$
	$	$	Total Expenses	$
	$	$	Remaining	$
Total	$	$	Total	$

Expenses

Expense	Budgeted	Amount	Expense	Budgeted	Amount
	$	$		$	$
	$	$		$	$
	$	$		$	$
	$	$		$	$
	$	$		$	$
	$	$		$	$
	$	$		$	$
	$	$		$	$
	$	$		$	$
Total	$	$	Total	$	$

Debt Repayment

Creditor	Balance	Paid
	$	$
	$	$
	$	$

Savings

Account	Goal	Amount
	$	$
	$	$

Income

Dates _____

Income Source	Budgeted	Amount	Remaining Income	Amount
	$	$	Total Income	$
	$	$	Total Expenses	$
	$	$	Remaining	$
Total	$	$	Total	$

Expenses

Expense	Budgeted	Amount	Expense	Budgeted	Amount
	$	$		$	$
	$	$		$	$
	$	$		$	$
	$	$		$	$
	$	$		$	$
	$	$		$	$
	$	$		$	$
	$	$		$	$
	$	$		$	$
Total	$	$	Total	$	$

Debt Repayment

Creditor	Balance	Paid
	$	$
	$	$
	$	$

Savings

Account	Goal	Amount
	$	$
	$	$

Income

Dates _____

Income Source	Budgeted	Amount	Remaining Income	Amount
	$	$	Total Income	$
	$	$	Total Expenses	$
	$	$	Remaining	$
Total	$	$	Total	$

Expenses

Expense	Budgeted	Amount	Expense	Budgeted	Amount
	$	$		$	$
	$	$		$	$
	$	$		$	$
	$	$		$	$
	$	$		$	$
	$	$		$	$
	$	$		$	$
	$	$		$	$
	$	$		$	$
Total	$	$	Total	$	$

Debt Repayment

Creditor	Balance	Paid
	$	$
	$	$
	$	$

Savings

Account	Goal	Amount
	$	$
	$	$

Income

Dates _____

Income Source	Budgeted	Amount	Remaining Income	Amount
	$	$	Total Income	$
	$	$	Total Expenses	$
	$	$	Remaining	$
Total	$	$	Total	$

Expenses

Expense	Budgeted	Amount	Expense	Budgeted	Amount
	$	$		$	$
	$	$		$	$
	$	$		$	$
	$	$		$	$
	$	$		$	$
	$	$		$	$
	$	$		$	$
	$	$		$	$
	$	$		$	$
Total	$	$	Total	$	$

Debt Repayment

Creditor	Balance	Paid
	$	$
	$	$
	$	$

Savings

Account	Goal	Amount
	$	$
	$	$

Income

Dates _____

Income Source	Budgeted	Amount	Remaining Income	Amount
	$	$	Total Income	$
	$	$	Total Expenses	$
	$	$	Remaining	$
Total	$	$	Total	$

Expenses

Expense	Budgeted	Amount	Expense	Budgeted	Amount
	$	$		$	$
	$	$		$	$
	$	$		$	$
	$	$		$	$
	$	$		$	$
	$	$		$	$
	$	$		$	$
	$	$		$	$
	$	$		$	$
Total	$	$	Total	$	$

Debt Repayment

Creditor	Balance	Paid
	$	$
	$	$
	$	$

Savings

Account	Goal	Amount
	$	$
	$	$

Income

Dates _____

Income Source	Budgeted	Amount	Remaining Income	Amount
	$	$	Total Income	$
	$	$	Total Expenses	$
	$	$	Remaining	$
Total	$	$	Total	$

Expenses

Expense	Budgeted	Amount	Expense	Budgeted	Amount
	$	$		$	$
	$	$		$	$
	$	$		$	$
	$	$		$	$
	$	$		$	$
	$	$		$	$
	$	$		$	$
	$	$		$	$
	$	$		$	$
Total	$	$	Total	$	$

Debt Repayment

Creditor	Balance	Paid
	$	$
	$	$
	$	$

Savings

Account	Goal	Amount
	$	$
	$	$

Income

Dates _____

Income Source	Budgeted	Amount	Remaining Income	Amount
	$	$	Total Income	$
	$	$	Total Expenses	$
	$	$	Remaining	$
Total	$	$	Total	$

Expenses

Expense	Budgeted	Amount	Expense	Budgeted	Amount
	$	$		$	$
	$	$		$	$
	$	$		$	$
	$	$		$	$
	$	$		$	$
	$	$		$	$
	$	$		$	$
	$	$		$	$
	$	$		$	$
Total	$	$	Total	$	$

Debt Repayment

Creditor	Balance	Paid
	$	$
	$	$
	$	$

Savings

Account	Goal	Amount
	$	$
	$	$

Income

Dates _____

Income Source	Budgeted	Amount	Remaining Income	Amount
	$	$	Total Income	$
	$	$	Total Expenses	$
	$	$	Remaining	$
Total	$	$	Total	$

Expenses

Expense	Budgeted	Amount	Expense	Budgeted	Amount
	$	$		$	$
	$	$		$	$
	$	$		$	$
	$	$		$	$
	$	$		$	$
	$	$		$	$
	$	$		$	$
	$	$		$	$
	$	$		$	$
Total	$	$	Total	$	$

Debt Repayment

Creditor	Balance	Paid
	$	$
	$	$
	$	$

Savings

Account	Goal	Amount
	$	$
	$	$

Income

Dates _____

Income Source	Budgeted	Amount	Remaining Income	Amount
	$	$	Total Income	$
	$	$	Total Expenses	$
	$	$	Remaining	$
Total	$	$	Total	$

Expenses

Expense	Budgeted	Amount	Expense	Budgeted	Amount
	$	$		$	$
	$	$		$	$
	$	$		$	$
	$	$		$	$
	$	$		$	$
	$	$		$	$
	$	$		$	$
	$	$		$	$
	$	$		$	$
Total	$	$	Total	$	$

Debt Repayment

Creditor	Balance	Paid
	$	$
	$	$
	$	$

Savings

Account	Goal	Amount
	$	$
	$	$

Income

Dates _____

Income Source	Budgeted	Amount	Remaining Income	Amount
	$	$	Total Income	$
	$	$	Total Expenses	$
	$	$	Remaining	$
Total	$	$	Total	$

Expenses

Expense	Budgeted	Amount	Expense	Budgeted	Amount
	$	$		$	$
	$	$		$	$
	$	$		$	$
	$	$		$	$
	$	$		$	$
	$	$		$	$
	$	$		$	$
	$	$		$	$
	$	$		$	$
Total	$	$	Total	$	$

Debt Repayment

Creditor	Balance	Paid
	$	$
	$	$
	$	$

Savings

Account	Goal	Amount
	$	$
	$	$

Income

Dates _____

Income Source	Budgeted	Amount	Remaining Income	Amount
	$	$	Total Income	$
	$	$	Total Expenses	$
	$	$	Remaining	$
Total	$	$	Total	$

Expenses

Expense	Budgeted	Amount	Expense	Budgeted	Amount
	$	$		$	$
	$	$		$	$
	$	$		$	$
	$	$		$	$
	$	$		$	$
	$	$		$	$
	$	$		$	$
	$	$		$	$
	$	$		$	$
Total	$	$	Total	$	$

Debt Repayment

Creditor	Balance	Paid
	$	$
	$	$
	$	$

Savings

Account	Goal	Amount
	$	$
	$	$

Income

Dates _____

Income Source	Budgeted	Amount	Remaining Income	Amount
	$	$	Total Income	$
	$	$	Total Expenses	$
	$	$	Remaining	$
Total	$	$	Total	$

Expenses

Expense	Budgeted	Amount	Expense	Budgeted	Amount
	$	$		$	$
	$	$		$	$
	$	$		$	$
	$	$		$	$
	$	$		$	$
	$	$		$	$
	$	$		$	$
	$	$		$	$
	$	$		$	$
Total	$	$	Total	$	$

Debt Repayment

Creditor	Balance	Paid
	$	$
	$	$
	$	$

Savings

Account	Goal	Amount
	$	$
	$	$

Income

Dates _____

Income Source	Budgeted	Amount	Remaining Income	Amount
	$	$	Total Income	$
	$	$	Total Expenses	$
	$	$	Remaining	$
Total	$	$	Total	$

Expenses

Expense	Budgeted	Amount	Expense	Budgeted	Amount
	$	$		$	$
	$	$		$	$
	$	$		$	$
	$	$		$	$
	$	$		$	$
	$	$		$	$
	$	$		$	$
	$	$		$	$
	$	$		$	$
Total	$	$	Total	$	$

Debt Repayment

Creditor	Balance	Paid
	$	$
	$	$
	$	$

Savings

Account	Goal	Amount
	$	$
	$	$

Income

Dates _____

Income Source	Budgeted	Amount	Remaining Income	Amount
	$	$	Total Income	$
	$	$	Total Expenses	$
	$	$	Remaining	$
Total	$	$	Total	$

Expenses

Expense	Budgeted	Amount	Expense	Budgeted	Amount
	$	$		$	$
	$	$		$	$
	$	$		$	$
	$	$		$	$
	$	$		$	$
	$	$		$	$
	$	$		$	$
	$	$		$	$
	$	$		$	$
Total	$	$	Total	$	$

Debt Repayment

Creditor	Balance	Paid
	$	$
	$	$
	$	$

Savings

Account	Goal	Amount
	$	$
	$	$

Income

Dates _____

Income Source	Budgeted	Amount	Remaining Income	Amount
	$	$	Total Income	$
	$	$	Total Expenses	$
	$	$	Remaining	$
Total	$	$	Total	$

Expenses

Expense	Budgeted	Amount	Expense	Budgeted	Amount
	$	$		$	$
	$	$		$	$
	$	$		$	$
	$	$		$	$
	$	$		$	$
	$	$		$	$
	$	$		$	$
	$	$		$	$
	$	$		$	$
Total	$	$	Total	$	$

Debt Repayment

Creditor	Balance	Paid
	$	$
	$	$
	$	$

Savings

Account	Goal	Amount
	$	$
	$	$

Income

Dates _____

Income Source	Budgeted	Amount	Remaining Income	Amount
	$	$	Total Income	$
	$	$	Total Expenses	$
	$	$	Remaining	$
Total	$	$	Total	$

Expenses

Expense	Budgeted	Amount	Expense	Budgeted	Amount
	$	$		$	$
	$	$		$	$
	$	$		$	$
	$	$		$	$
	$	$		$	$
	$	$		$	$
	$	$		$	$
	$	$		$	$
	$	$		$	$
Total	$	$	Total	$	$

Debt Repayment

Creditor	Balance	Paid
	$	$
	$	$
	$	$

Savings

Account	Goal	Amount
	$	$
	$	$

Income

Dates _____

Income Source	Budgeted	Amount	Remaining Income	Amount
	$	$	Total Income	$
	$	$	Total Expenses	$
	$	$	Remaining	$
Total	$	$	Total	$

Expenses

Expense	Budgeted	Amount	Expense	Budgeted	Amount
	$	$		$	$
	$	$		$	$
	$	$		$	$
	$	$		$	$
	$	$		$	$
	$	$		$	$
	$	$		$	$
	$	$		$	$
	$	$		$	$
Total	$	$	Total	$	$

Debt Repayment

Creditor	Balance	Paid
	$	$
	$	$
	$	$

Savings

Account	Goal	Amount
	$	$
	$	$

Income

Dates _____

Income Source	Budgeted	Amount	Remaining Income	Amount
	$	$	Total Income	$
	$	$	Total Expenses	$
	$	$	Remaining	$
Total	$	$	Total	$

Expenses

Expense	Budgeted	Amount	Expense	Budgeted	Amount
	$	$		$	$
	$	$		$	$
	$	$		$	$
	$	$		$	$
	$	$		$	$
	$	$		$	$
	$	$		$	$
	$	$		$	$
	$	$		$	$
Total	$	$	Total	$	$

Debt Repayment

Creditor	Balance	Paid
	$	$
	$	$
	$	$

Savings

Account	Goal	Amount
	$	$
	$	$

Income

Dates _____

Income Source	Budgeted	Amount	Remaining Income	Amount
	$	$	Total Income	$
	$	$	Total Expenses	$
	$	$	Remaining	$
Total	$	$	Total	$

Expenses

Expense	Budgeted	Amount	Expense	Budgeted	Amount
	$	$		$	$
	$	$		$	$
	$	$		$	$
	$	$		$	$
	$	$		$	$
	$	$		$	$
	$	$		$	$
	$	$		$	$
	$	$		$	$
Total	$	$	Total	$	$

Debt Repayment

Creditor	Balance	Paid
	$	$
	$	$
	$	$

Savings

Account	Goal	Amount
	$	$
	$	$

Income

Dates _____

Income Source	Budgeted	Amount	Remaining Income	Amount
	$	$	Total Income	$
	$	$	Total Expenses	$
	$	$	Remaining	$
Total	$	$	Total	$

Expenses

Expense	Budgeted	Amount	Expense	Budgeted	Amount
	$	$		$	$
	$	$		$	$
	$	$		$	$
	$	$		$	$
	$	$		$	$
	$	$		$	$
	$	$		$	$
	$	$		$	$
	$	$		$	$
Total	$	$	Total	$	$

Debt Repayment

Creditor	Balance	Paid
	$	$
	$	$
	$	$

Savings

Account	Goal	Amount
	$	$
	$	$

Income

Dates _____

Income Source	Budgeted	Amount	Remaining Income	Amount
	$	$	Total Income	$
	$	$	Total Expenses	$
	$	$	Remaining	$
Total	$	$	Total	$

Expenses

Expense	Budgeted	Amount	Expense	Budgeted	Amount
	$	$		$	$
	$	$		$	$
	$	$		$	$
	$	$		$	$
	$	$		$	$
	$	$		$	$
	$	$		$	$
	$	$		$	$
	$	$		$	$
Total	$	$	Total	$	$

Debt Repayment

Creditor	Balance	Paid
	$	$
	$	$
	$	$

Savings

Account	Goal	Amount
	$	$
	$	$

Income

Dates _____

Income Source	Budgeted	Amount	Remaining Income	Amount
	$	$	Total Income	$
	$	$	Total Expenses	$
	$	$	Remaining	$
Total	$	$	Total	$

Expenses

Expense	Budgeted	Amount	Expense	Budgeted	Amount
	$	$		$	$
	$	$		$	$
	$	$		$	$
	$	$		$	$
	$	$		$	$
	$	$		$	$
	$	$		$	$
	$	$		$	$
	$	$		$	$
Total	$	$	Total	$	$

Debt Repayment

Creditor	Balance	Paid
	$	$
	$	$
	$	$

Savings

Account	Goal	Amount
	$	$
	$	$

Income

Dates _____

Income Source	Budgeted	Amount	Remaining Income	Amount
	$	$	Total Income	$
	$	$	Total Expenses	$
	$	$	Remaining	$
Total	$	$	Total	$

Expenses

Expense	Budgeted	Amount	Expense	Budgeted	Amount
	$	$		$	$
	$	$		$	$
	$	$		$	$
	$	$		$	$
	$	$		$	$
	$	$		$	$
	$	$		$	$
	$	$		$	$
	$	$		$	$
Total	$	$	Total	$	$

Debt Repayment

Creditor	Balance	Paid
	$	$
	$	$
	$	$

Savings

Account	Goal	Amount
	$	$
	$	$

Income

Dates _____

Income Source	Budgeted	Amount	Remaining Income	Amount
	$	$	Total Income	$
	$	$	Total Expenses	$
	$	$	Remaining	$
Total	$	$	Total	$

Expenses

Expense	Budgeted	Amount	Expense	Budgeted	Amount
	$	$		$	$
	$	$		$	$
	$	$		$	$
	$	$		$	$
	$	$		$	$
	$	$		$	$
	$	$		$	$
	$	$		$	$
	$	$		$	$
Total	$	$	Total	$	$

Debt Repayment

Creditor	Balance	Paid
	$	$
	$	$
	$	$

Savings

Account	Goal	Amount
	$	$
	$	$

Income

Dates _____

Income Source	Budgeted	Amount	Remaining Income	Amount
	$	$	Total Income	$
	$	$	Total Expenses	$
	$	$	Remaining	$
Total	$	$	Total	$

Expenses

Expense	Budgeted	Amount	Expense	Budgeted	Amount
	$	$		$	$
	$	$		$	$
	$	$		$	$
	$	$		$	$
	$	$		$	$
	$	$		$	$
	$	$		$	$
	$	$		$	$
	$	$		$	$
Total	$	$	Total	$	$

Debt Repayment

Creditor	Balance	Paid
	$	$
	$	$
	$	$

Savings

Account	Goal	Amount
	$	$
	$	$

Income

Dates _____

Income Source	Budgeted	Amount	Remaining Income	Amount
	$	$	Total Income	$
	$	$	Total Expenses	$
	$	$	Remaining	$
Total	$	$	Total	$

Expenses

Expense	Budgeted	Amount	Expense	Budgeted	Amount
	$	$		$	$
	$	$		$	$
	$	$		$	$
	$	$		$	$
	$	$		$	$
	$	$		$	$
	$	$		$	$
	$	$		$	$
	$	$		$	$
Total	$	$	Total	$	$

Debt Repayment

Creditor	Balance	Paid
	$	$
	$	$
	$	$

Savings

Account	Goal	Amount
	$	$
	$	$

Income

Dates _____

Income Source	Budgeted	Amount	Remaining Income	Amount
	$	$	Total Income	$
	$	$	Total Expenses	$
	$	$	Remaining	$
Total	$	$	Total	$

Expenses

Expense	Budgeted	Amount	Expense	Budgeted	Amount
	$	$		$	$
	$	$		$	$
	$	$		$	$
	$	$		$	$
	$	$		$	$
	$	$		$	$
	$	$		$	$
	$	$		$	$
	$	$		$	$
Total	$	$	Total	$	$

Debt Repayment

Creditor	Balance	Paid
	$	$
	$	$
	$	$

Savings

Account	Goal	Amount
	$	$
	$	$

Income

Dates _____

Income Source	Budgeted	Amount	Remaining Income	Amount
	$	$	Total Income	$
	$	$	Total Expenses	$
	$	$	Remaining	$
Total	$	$	Total	$

Expenses

Expense	Budgeted	Amount	Expense	Budgeted	Amount
	$	$		$	$
	$	$		$	$
	$	$		$	$
	$	$		$	$
	$	$		$	$
	$	$		$	$
	$	$		$	$
	$	$		$	$
	$	$		$	$
Total	$	$	Total	$	$

Debt Repayment

Creditor	Balance	Paid
	$	$
	$	$
	$	$

Savings

Account	Goal	Amount
	$	$
	$	$

Income

Dates _____

Income Source	Budgeted	Amount	Remaining Income	Amount
	$	$	Total Income	$
	$	$	Total Expenses	$
	$	$	Remaining	$
Total	$	$	Total	$

Expenses

Expense	Budgeted	Amount	Expense	Budgeted	Amount
	$	$		$	$
	$	$		$	$
	$	$		$	$
	$	$		$	$
	$	$		$	$
	$	$		$	$
	$	$		$	$
	$	$		$	$
	$	$		$	$
Total	$	$	Total	$	$

Debt Repayment

Creditor	Balance	Paid
	$	$
	$	$
	$	$

Savings

Account	Goal	Amount
	$	$
	$	$

Income

Dates _____

Income Source	Budgeted	Amount	Remaining Income	Amount
	$	$	Total Income	$
	$	$	Total Expenses	$
	$	$	Remaining	$
Total	$	$	Total	$

Expenses

Expense	Budgeted	Amount	Expense	Budgeted	Amount
	$	$		$	$
	$	$		$	$
	$	$		$	$
	$	$		$	$
	$	$		$	$
	$	$		$	$
	$	$		$	$
	$	$		$	$
	$	$		$	$
Total	$	$	Total	$	$

Debt Repayment

Creditor	Balance	Paid
	$	$
	$	$
	$	$

Savings

Account	Goal	Amount
	$	$
	$	$

Dates _____

Income

Income Source	Budgeted	Amount	Remaining Income	Amount
	$	$	Total Income	$
	$	$	Total Expenses	$
	$	$	Remaining	$
Total	$	$	Total	$

Expenses

Expense	Budgeted	Amount	Expense	Budgeted	Amount
	$	$		$	$
	$	$		$	$
	$	$		$	$
	$	$		$	$
	$	$		$	$
	$	$		$	$
	$	$		$	$
	$	$		$	$
	$	$		$	$
Total	$	$	Total	$	$

Debt Repayment

Creditor	Balance	Paid
	$	$
	$	$
	$	$

Savings

Account	Goal	Amount
	$	$
	$	$

Income

Dates _____

Income Source	Budgeted	Amount	Remaining Income	Amount
	$	$	Total Income	$
	$	$	Total Expenses	$
	$	$	Remaining	$
Total	$	$	Total	$

Expenses

Expense	Budgeted	Amount	Expense	Budgeted	Amount
	$	$		$	$
	$	$		$	$
	$	$		$	$
	$	$		$	$
	$	$		$	$
	$	$		$	$
	$	$		$	$
	$	$		$	$
	$	$		$	$
Total	$	$	Total	$	$

Debt Repayment

Creditor	Balance	Paid
	$	$
	$	$
	$	$

Savings

Account	Goal	Amount
	$	$
	$	$

Income

Dates _____

Income Source	Budgeted	Amount	Remaining Income	Amount
	$	$	Total Income	$
	$	$	Total Expenses	$
	$	$	Remaining	$
Total	$	$	Total	$

Expenses

Expense	Budgeted	Amount	Expense	Budgeted	Amount
	$	$		$	$
	$	$		$	$
	$	$		$	$
	$	$		$	$
	$	$		$	$
	$	$		$	$
	$	$		$	$
	$	$		$	$
	$	$		$	$
Total	$	$	Total	$	$

Debt Repayment

Creditor	Balance	Paid
	$	$
	$	$
	$	$

Savings

Account	Goal	Amount
	$	$
	$	$

Income

Dates _____

Income Source	Budgeted	Amount	Remaining Income	Amount
	$	$	Total Income	$
	$	$	Total Expenses	$
	$	$	Remaining	$
Total	$	$	Total	$

Expenses

Expense	Budgeted	Amount	Expense	Budgeted	Amount
	$	$		$	$
	$	$		$	$
	$	$		$	$
	$	$		$	$
	$	$		$	$
	$	$		$	$
	$	$		$	$
	$	$		$	$
	$	$		$	$
Total	$	$	Total	$	$

Debt Repayment

Creditor	Balance	Paid
	$	$
	$	$
	$	$

Savings

Account	Goal	Amount
	$	$
	$	$

Income

Dates _____

Income Source	Budgeted	Amount	Remaining Income	Amount
	$	$	Total Income	$
	$	$	Total Expenses	$
	$	$	Remaining	$
Total	$	$	Total	$

Expenses

Expense	Budgeted	Amount	Expense	Budgeted	Amount
	$	$		$	$
	$	$		$	$
	$	$		$	$
	$	$		$	$
	$	$		$	$
	$	$		$	$
	$	$		$	$
	$	$		$	$
	$	$		$	$
Total	$	$	Total	$	$

Debt Repayment

Creditor	Balance	Paid
	$	$
	$	$
	$	$

Savings

Account	Goal	Amount
	$	$
	$	$

Income

Dates _____

Income Source	Budgeted	Amount	Remaining Income	Amount
	$	$	Total Income	$
	$	$	Total Expenses	$
	$	$	Remaining	$
Total	$	$	Total	$

Expenses

Expense	Budgeted	Amount	Expense	Budgeted	Amount
	$	$		$	$
	$	$		$	$
	$	$		$	$
	$	$		$	$
	$	$		$	$
	$	$		$	$
	$	$		$	$
	$	$		$	$
	$	$		$	$
Total	$	$	Total	$	$

Debt Repayment

Creditor	Balance	Paid
	$	$
	$	$
	$	$

Savings

Account	Goal	Amount
	$	$
	$	$

Income

Dates _____

Income Source	Budgeted	Amount	Remaining Income	Amount
	$	$	Total Income	$
	$	$	Total Expenses	$
	$	$	Remaining	$
Total	$	$	Total	$

Expenses

Expense	Budgeted	Amount	Expense	Budgeted	Amount
	$	$		$	$
	$	$		$	$
	$	$		$	$
	$	$		$	$
	$	$		$	$
	$	$		$	$
	$	$		$	$
	$	$		$	$
	$	$		$	$
Total	$	$	Total	$	$

Debt Repayment

Creditor	Balance	Paid
	$	$
	$	$
	$	$

Savings

Account	Goal	Amount
	$	$
	$	$

Income

Dates _____

Income Source	Budgeted	Amount	Remaining Income	Amount
	$	$	Total Income	$
	$	$	Total Expenses	$
	$	$	Remaining	$
Total	$	$	Total	$

Expenses

Expense	Budgeted	Amount	Expense	Budgeted	Amount
	$	$		$	$
	$	$		$	$
	$	$		$	$
	$	$		$	$
	$	$		$	$
	$	$		$	$
	$	$		$	$
	$	$		$	$
	$	$		$	$
Total	$	$	Total	$	$

Debt Repayment

Creditor	Balance	Paid
	$	$
	$	$
	$	$

Savings

Account	Goal	Amount
	$	$
	$	$

Income

Dates _____

Income Source	Budgeted	Amount	Remaining Income	Amount
	$	$	Total Income	$
	$	$	Total Expenses	$
	$	$	Remaining	$
Total	$	$	Total	$

Expenses

Expense	Budgeted	Amount	Expense	Budgeted	Amount
	$	$		$	$
	$	$		$	$
	$	$		$	$
	$	$		$	$
	$	$		$	$
	$	$		$	$
	$	$		$	$
	$	$		$	$
	$	$		$	$
Total	$	$	Total	$	$

Debt Repayment

Creditor	Balance	Paid
	$	$
	$	$
	$	$

Savings

Account	Goal	Amount
	$	$
	$	$

Income

Dates _____

Income Source	Budgeted	Amount	Remaining Income	Amount
	$	$	Total Income	$
	$	$	Total Expenses	$
	$	$	Remaining	$
Total	$	$	Total	$

Expenses

Expense	Budgeted	Amount	Expense	Budgeted	Amount
	$	$		$	$
	$	$		$	$
	$	$		$	$
	$	$		$	$
	$	$		$	$
	$	$		$	$
	$	$		$	$
	$	$		$	$
	$	$		$	$
Total	$	$	Total	$	$

Debt Repayment

Creditor	Balance	Paid
	$	$
	$	$
	$	$

Savings

Account	Goal	Amount
	$	$
	$	$

Income

Dates _____

Income Source	Budgeted	Amount	Remaining Income	Amount
	$	$	Total Income	$
	$	$	Total Expenses	$
	$	$	Remaining	$
Total	$	$	Total	$

Expenses

Expense	Budgeted	Amount	Expense	Budgeted	Amount
	$	$		$	$
	$	$		$	$
	$	$		$	$
	$	$		$	$
	$	$		$	$
	$	$		$	$
	$	$		$	$
	$	$		$	$
	$	$		$	$
Total	$	$	Total	$	$

Debt Repayment

Creditor		Balance	Paid
		$	$
		$	$
		$	$

Savings

Account		Goal	Amount
		$	$
		$	$

Income

Dates _____

Income Source	Budgeted	Amount	Remaining Income	Amount
	$	$	Total Income	$
	$	$	Total Expenses	$
	$	$	Remaining	$
Total	$	$	Total	$

Expenses

Expense	Budgeted	Amount	Expense	Budgeted	Amount
	$	$		$	$
	$	$		$	$
	$	$		$	$
	$	$		$	$
	$	$		$	$
	$	$		$	$
	$	$		$	$
	$	$		$	$
	$	$		$	$
Total	$	$	Total	$	$

Debt Repayment

Creditor	Balance	Paid
	$	$
	$	$
	$	$

Savings

Account	Goal	Amount
	$	$
	$	$

Income

Dates _____

Income Source	Budgeted	Amount	Remaining Income	Amount
	$	$	Total Income	$
	$	$	Total Expenses	$
	$	$	Remaining	$
Total	$	$	Total	$

Expenses

Expense	Budgeted	Amount	Expense	Budgeted	Amount
	$	$		$	$
	$	$		$	$
	$	$		$	$
	$	$		$	$
	$	$		$	$
	$	$		$	$
	$	$		$	$
	$	$		$	$
	$	$		$	$
Total	$	$	Total	$	$

Debt Repayment

Creditor	Balance	Paid
	$	$
	$	$
	$	$

Savings

Account	Goal	Amount
	$	$
	$	$

Income

Dates _____

Income Source	Budgeted	Amount	Remaining Income	Amount
	$	$	Total Income	$
	$	$	Total Expenses	$
	$	$	Remaining	$
Total	$	$	Total	$

Expenses

Expense	Budgeted	Amount	Expense	Budgeted	Amount
	$	$		$	$
	$	$		$	$
	$	$		$	$
	$	$		$	$
	$	$		$	$
	$	$		$	$
	$	$		$	$
	$	$		$	$
	$	$		$	$
Total	$	$	Total	$	$

Debt Repayment

Creditor	Balance	Paid
	$	$
	$	$
	$	$

Savings

Account	Goal	Amount
	$	$
	$	$

Income

Dates _____

Income Source	Budgeted	Amount	Remaining Income	Amount
	$	$	Total Income	$
	$	$	Total Expenses	$
	$	$	Remaining	$
Total	$	$	Total	$

Expenses

Expense	Budgeted	Amount	Expense	Budgeted	Amount
	$	$		$	$
	$	$		$	$
	$	$		$	$
	$	$		$	$
	$	$		$	$
	$	$		$	$
	$	$		$	$
	$	$		$	$
	$	$		$	$
Total	$	$	Total	$	$

Debt Repayment

Creditor	Balance	Paid
	$	$
	$	$
	$	$

Savings

Account	Goal	Amount
	$	$
	$	$

Income

Dates _____

Income Source	Budgeted	Amount	Remaining Income	Amount
	$	$	Total Income	$
	$	$	Total Expenses	$
	$	$	Remaining	$
Total	$	$	Total	$

Expenses

Expense	Budgeted	Amount	Expense	Budgeted	Amount
	$	$		$	$
	$	$		$	$
	$	$		$	$
	$	$		$	$
	$	$		$	$
	$	$		$	$
	$	$		$	$
	$	$		$	$
	$	$		$	$
Total	$	$	Total	$	$

Debt Repayment

Creditor	Balance	Paid
	$	$
	$	$
	$	$

Savings

Account	Goal	Amount
	$	$
	$	$

Income

Dates _____

Income Source	Budgeted	Amount	Remaining Income	Amount
	$	$	Total Income	$
	$	$	Total Expenses	$
	$	$	Remaining	$
Total	$	$	Total	$

Expenses

Expense	Budgeted	Amount	Expense	Budgeted	Amount
	$	$		$	$
	$	$		$	$
	$	$		$	$
	$	$		$	$
	$	$		$	$
	$	$		$	$
	$	$		$	$
	$	$		$	$
	$	$		$	$
Total	$	$	Total	$	$

Debt Repayment

Creditor	Balance	Paid
	$	$
	$	$
	$	$

Savings

Account	Goal	Amount
	$	$
	$	$

Income

Dates _____

Income Source	Budgeted	Amount	Remaining Income	Amount
	$	$	Total Income	$
	$	$	Total Expenses	$
	$	$	Remaining	$
Total	$	$	Total	$

Expenses

Expense	Budgeted	Amount	Expense	Budgeted	Amount
	$	$		$	$
	$	$		$	$
	$	$		$	$
	$	$		$	$
	$	$		$	$
	$	$		$	$
	$	$		$	$
	$	$		$	$
	$	$		$	$
Total	$	$	Total	$	$

Debt Repayment

Creditor	Balance	Paid
	$	$
	$	$
	$	$

Savings

Account	Goal	Amount
	$	$
	$	$

Income

Dates _____

Income Source	Budgeted	Amount	Remaining Income	Amount
	$	$	Total Income	$
	$	$	Total Expenses	$
	$	$	Remaining	$
Total	$	$	Total	$

Expenses

Expense	Budgeted	Amount	Expense	Budgeted	Amount
	$	$		$	$
	$	$		$	$
	$	$		$	$
	$	$		$	$
	$	$		$	$
	$	$		$	$
	$	$		$	$
	$	$		$	$
	$	$		$	$
Total	$	$	Total	$	$

Debt Repayment

Creditor	Balance	Paid
	$	$
	$	$
	$	$

Savings

Account	Goal	Amount
	$	$
	$	$

Income

Dates _____

Income Source	Budgeted	Amount	Remaining Income	Amount
	$	$	Total Income	$
	$	$	Total Expenses	$
	$	$	Remaining	$
Total	$	$	Total	$

Expenses

Expense	Budgeted	Amount	Expense	Budgeted	Amount
	$	$		$	$
	$	$		$	$
	$	$		$	$
	$	$		$	$
	$	$		$	$
	$	$		$	$
	$	$		$	$
	$	$		$	$
	$	$		$	$
Total	$	$	Total	$	$

Debt Repayment

Creditor	Balance	Paid
	$	$
	$	$
	$	$

Savings

Account	Goal	Amount
	$	$
	$	$

Income

Dates _____

Income Source	Budgeted	Amount	Remaining Income	Amount
	$	$	Total Income	$
	$	$	Total Expenses	$
	$	$	Remaining	$
Total	$	$	Total	$

Expenses

Expense	Budgeted	Amount	Expense	Budgeted	Amount
	$	$		$	$
	$	$		$	$
	$	$		$	$
	$	$		$	$
	$	$		$	$
	$	$		$	$
	$	$		$	$
	$	$		$	$
	$	$		$	$
	$	$		$	$
Total	$	$	Total	$	$

Debt Repayment

Creditor	Balance	Paid
	$	$
	$	$
	$	$

Savings

Account	Goal	Amount
	$	$
	$	$

Income

Dates _____

Income Source	Budgeted	Amount	Remaining Income	Amount
	$	$	Total Income	$
	$	$	Total Expenses	$
	$	$	Remaining	$
Total	$	$	Total	$

Expenses

Expense	Budgeted	Amount	Expense	Budgeted	Amount
	$	$		$	$
	$	$		$	$
	$	$		$	$
	$	$		$	$
	$	$		$	$
	$	$		$	$
	$	$		$	$
	$	$		$	$
	$	$		$	$
Total	$	$	Total	$	$

Debt Repayment

Creditor	Balance	Paid
	$	$
	$	$
	$	$

Savings

Account	Goal	Amount
	$	$
	$	$

Income

Dates _____

Income Source	Budgeted	Amount	Remaining Income	Amount
	$	$	Total Income	$
	$	$	Total Expenses	$
	$	$	Remaining	$
Total	$	$	Total	$

Expenses

Expense	Budgeted	Amount	Expense	Budgeted	Amount
	$	$		$	$
	$	$		$	$
	$	$		$	$
	$	$		$	$
	$	$		$	$
	$	$		$	$
	$	$		$	$
	$	$		$	$
	$	$		$	$
Total	$	$	Total	$	$

Debt Repayment

Creditor			Balance	Paid
			$	$
			$	$
			$	$

Savings

Account			Goal	Amount
			$	$
			$	$

Income

Dates _____

Income Source	Budgeted	Amount	Remaining Income		Amount
	$	$	Total Income		$
	$	$	Total Expenses		$
	$	$	Remaining		$
Total	$	$	Total		$

Expenses

Expense	Budgeted	Amount	Expense	Budgeted	Amount
	$	$		$	$
	$	$		$	$
	$	$		$	$
	$	$		$	$
	$	$		$	$
	$	$		$	$
	$	$		$	$
	$	$		$	$
	$	$		$	$
Total	$	$	Total	$	$

Debt Repayment

Creditor	Balance	Paid
	$	$
	$	$
	$	$

Savings

Account	Goal	Amount
	$	$
	$	$

Income

Dates _____

Income Source	Budgeted	Amount	Remaining Income	Amount
	$	$	Total Income	$
	$	$	Total Expenses	$
	$	$	Remaining	$
Total	$	$	Total	$

Expenses

Expense	Budgeted	Amount	Expense	Budgeted	Amount
	$	$		$	$
	$	$		$	$
	$	$		$	$
	$	$		$	$
	$	$		$	$
	$	$		$	$
	$	$		$	$
	$	$		$	$
	$	$		$	$
Total	$	$	Total	$	$

Debt Repayment

Creditor	Balance	Paid
	$	$
	$	$
	$	$

Savings

Account	Goal	Amount
	$	$
	$	$

Income

Dates _____

Income Source	Budgeted	Amount	Remaining Income	Amount
	$	$	Total Income	$
	$	$	Total Expenses	$
	$	$	Remaining	$
Total	$	$	Total	$

Expenses

Expense	Budgeted	Amount	Expense	Budgeted	Amount
	$	$		$	$
	$	$		$	$
	$	$		$	$
	$	$		$	$
	$	$		$	$
	$	$		$	$
	$	$		$	$
	$	$		$	$
	$	$		$	$
Total	$	$	Total	$	$

Debt Repayment

Creditor	Balance	Paid
	$	$
	$	$
	$	$

Savings

Account	Goal	Amount
	$	$
	$	$

Dates _____

Income

Income Source	Budgeted	Amount
	$	$
	$	$
	$	$
Total	$	$

Remaining Income	Amount
Total Income	$
Total Expenses	$
Remaining	$
Total	$

Expenses

Expense	Budgeted	Amount
	$	$
	$	$
	$	$
	$	$
	$	$
	$	$
	$	$
	$	$
	$	$
Total	$	$

Expense	Budgeted	Amount
	$	$
	$	$
	$	$
	$	$
	$	$
	$	$
	$	$
	$	$
	$	$
Total	$	$

Debt Repayment

Creditor	Balance	Paid
	$	$
	$	$
	$	$

Savings

Account	Goal	Amount
	$	$
	$	$

Income

Dates _____

Income Source	Budgeted	Amount	Remaining Income	Amount
	$	$	Total Income	$
	$	$	Total Expenses	$
	$	$	Remaining	$
Total	$	$	Total	$

Expenses

Expense	Budgeted	Amount	Expense	Budgeted	Amount
	$	$		$	$
	$	$		$	$
	$	$		$	$
	$	$		$	$
	$	$		$	$
	$	$		$	$
	$	$		$	$
	$	$		$	$
	$	$		$	$
Total	$	$	Total	$	$

Debt Repayment

Creditor	Balance	Paid
	$	$
	$	$
	$	$

Savings

Account	Goal	Amount
	$	$
	$	$

Income

Dates _____

Income Source	Budgeted	Amount	Remaining Income	Amount
	$	$	Total Income	$
	$	$	Total Expenses	$
	$	$	Remaining	$
Total	$	$	Total	$

Expenses

Expense	Budgeted	Amount	Expense	Budgeted	Amount
	$	$		$	$
	$	$		$	$
	$	$		$	$
	$	$		$	$
	$	$		$	$
	$	$		$	$
	$	$		$	$
	$	$		$	$
	$	$		$	$
Total	$	$	Total	$	$

Debt Repayment

Creditor	Balance	Paid
	$	$
	$	$
	$	$

Savings

Account	Goal	Amount
	$	$
	$	$

Income

Dates _____

Income Source	Budgeted	Amount	Remaining Income	Amount
	$	$	Total Income	$
	$	$	Total Expenses	$
	$	$	Remaining	$
Total	$	$	Total	$

Expenses

Expense	Budgeted	Amount	Expense	Budgeted	Amount
	$	$		$	$
	$	$		$	$
	$	$		$	$
	$	$		$	$
	$	$		$	$
	$	$		$	$
	$	$		$	$
	$	$		$	$
	$	$		$	$
Total	$	$	Total	$	$

Debt Repayment

Creditor	Balance	Paid
	$	$
	$	$
	$	$

Savings

Account	Goal	Amount
	$	$
	$	$

Income

Dates _____

Income Source	Budgeted	Amount	Remaining Income	Amount
	$	$	Total Income	$
	$	$	Total Expenses	$
	$	$	Remaining	$
Total	$	$	Total	$

Expenses

Expense	Budgeted	Amount	Expense	Budgeted	Amount
	$	$		$	$
	$	$		$	$
	$	$		$	$
	$	$		$	$
	$	$		$	$
	$	$		$	$
	$	$		$	$
	$	$		$	$
	$	$		$	$
Total	$	$	Total	$	$

Debt Repayment

Creditor	Balance	Paid
	$	$
	$	$
	$	$

Savings

Account	Goal	Amount
	$	$
	$	$

Income

Dates _____

Income Source	Budgeted	Amount	Remaining Income	Amount
	$	$	Total Income	$
	$	$	Total Expenses	$
	$	$	Remaining	$
Total	$	$	Total	$

Expenses

Expense	Budgeted	Amount	Expense	Budgeted	Amount
	$	$		$	$
	$	$		$	$
	$	$		$	$
	$	$		$	$
	$	$		$	$
	$	$		$	$
	$	$		$	$
	$	$		$	$
	$	$		$	$
Total	$	$	Total	$	$

Debt Repayment

Creditor	Balance	Paid
	$	$
	$	$
	$	$

Savings

Account	Goal	Amount
	$	$
	$	$

Income

Dates _____

Income Source	Budgeted	Amount	Remaining Income	Amount
	$	$	Total Income	$
	$	$	Total Expenses	$
	$	$	Remaining	$
Total	$	$	Total	$

Expenses

Expense	Budgeted	Amount	Expense	Budgeted	Amount
	$	$		$	$
	$	$		$	$
	$	$		$	$
	$	$		$	$
	$	$		$	$
	$	$		$	$
	$	$		$	$
	$	$		$	$
	$	$		$	$
Total	$	$	Total	$	$

Debt Repayment

Creditor	Balance	Paid
	$	$
	$	$
	$	$

Savings

Account	Goal	Amount
	$	$
	$	$

Income

Dates _____

Income Source	Budgeted	Amount	Remaining Income	Amount
	$	$	Total Income	$
	$	$	Total Expenses	$
	$	$	Remaining	$
Total	$	$	Total	$

Expenses

Expense	Budgeted	Amount	Expense	Budgeted	Amount
	$	$		$	$
	$	$		$	$
	$	$		$	$
	$	$		$	$
	$	$		$	$
	$	$		$	$
	$	$		$	$
	$	$		$	$
	$	$		$	$
Total	$	$	Total	$	$

Debt Repayment

Creditor	Balance	Paid
	$	$
	$	$
	$	$

Savings

Account	Goal	Amount
	$	$
	$	$

Income

Dates _____

Income Source	Budgeted	Amount	Remaining Income	Amount
	$	$	Total Income	$
	$	$	Total Expenses	$
	$	$	Remaining	$
Total	$	$	Total	$

Expenses

Expense	Budgeted	Amount	Expense	Budgeted	Amount
	$	$		$	$
	$	$		$	$
	$	$		$	$
	$	$		$	$
	$	$		$	$
	$	$		$	$
	$	$		$	$
	$	$		$	$
	$	$		$	$
Total	$	$	Total	$	$

Debt Repayment

Creditor	Balance	Paid
	$	$
	$	$
	$	$

Savings

Account	Goal	Amount
	$	$
	$	$

Income

Dates _____

Income Source	Budgeted	Amount	Remaining Income	Amount
	$	$	Total Income	$
	$	$	Total Expenses	$
	$	$	Remaining	$
Total	$	$	Total	$

Expenses

Expense	Budgeted	Amount	Expense	Budgeted	Amount
	$	$		$	$
	$	$		$	$
	$	$		$	$
	$	$		$	$
	$	$		$	$
	$	$		$	$
	$	$		$	$
	$	$		$	$
	$	$		$	$
Total	$	$	Total	$	$

Debt Repayment

Creditor	Balance	Paid
	$	$
	$	$
	$	$

Savings

Account	Goal	Amount
	$	$
	$	$

Income

Dates _____

Income Source	Budgeted	Amount	Remaining Income	Amount
	$	$	Total Income	$
	$	$	Total Expenses	$
	$	$	Remaining	$
Total	$	$	Total	$

Expenses

Expense	Budgeted	Amount	Expense	Budgeted	Amount
	$	$		$	$
	$	$		$	$
	$	$		$	$
	$	$		$	$
	$	$		$	$
	$	$		$	$
	$	$		$	$
	$	$		$	$
	$	$		$	$
Total	$	$	Total	$	$

Debt Repayment

Creditor	Balance	Paid
	$	$
	$	$
	$	$

Savings

Account	Goal	Amount
	$	$
	$	$

Income

Dates _____

Income Source	Budgeted	Amount	Remaining Income	Amount
	$	$	Total Income	$
	$	$	Total Expenses	$
	$	$	Remaining	$
Total	$	$	Total	$

Expenses

Expense	Budgeted	Amount	Expense	Budgeted	Amount
	$	$		$	$
	$	$		$	$
	$	$		$	$
	$	$		$	$
	$	$		$	$
	$	$		$	$
	$	$		$	$
	$	$		$	$
	$	$		$	$
Total	$	$	Total	$	$

Debt Repayment

Creditor	Balance	Paid
	$	$
	$	$
	$	$

Savings

Account	Goal	Amount
	$	$
	$	$

Income

Dates _____

Income Source	Budgeted	Amount	Remaining Income	Amount
	$	$	Total Income	$
	$	$	Total Expenses	$
	$	$	Remaining	$
Total	$	$	Total	$

Expenses

Expense	Budgeted	Amount	Expense	Budgeted	Amount
	$	$		$	$
	$	$		$	$
	$	$		$	$
	$	$		$	$
	$	$		$	$
	$	$		$	$
	$	$		$	$
	$	$		$	$
	$	$		$	$
Total	$	$	Total	$	$

Debt Repayment

Creditor	Balance	Paid
	$	$
	$	$
	$	$

Savings

Account	Goal	Amount
	$	$
	$	$

Income

Dates _____

Income Source	Budgeted	Amount	Remaining Income	Amount
	$	$	Total Income	$
	$	$	Total Expenses	$
	$	$	Remaining	$
Total	$	$	Total	$

Expenses

Expense	Budgeted	Amount	Expense	Budgeted	Amount
	$	$		$	$
	$	$		$	$
	$	$		$	$
	$	$		$	$
	$	$		$	$
	$	$		$	$
	$	$		$	$
	$	$		$	$
	$	$		$	$
Total	$	$	Total	$	$

Debt Repayment

Creditor	Balance	Paid
	$	$
	$	$
	$	$

Savings

Account	Goal	Amount
	$	$
	$	$

Income

Dates _____

Income Source	Budgeted	Amount	Remaining Income	Amount
	$	$	Total Income	$
	$	$	Total Expenses	$
	$	$	Remaining	$
Total	$	$	Total	$

Expenses

Expense	Budgeted	Amount	Expense	Budgeted	Amount
	$	$		$	$
	$	$		$	$
	$	$		$	$
	$	$		$	$
	$	$		$	$
	$	$		$	$
	$	$		$	$
	$	$		$	$
	$	$		$	$
Total	$	$	Total	$	$

Debt Repayment

Creditor	Balance	Paid
	$	$
	$	$
	$	$

Savings

Account	Goal	Amount
	$	$
	$	$

Income

Dates _____

Income Source	Budgeted	Amount	Remaining Income	Amount
	$	$	Total Income	$
	$	$	Total Expenses	$
	$	$	Remaining	$
Total	$	$	Total	$

Expenses

Expense	Budgeted	Amount	Expense	Budgeted	Amount
	$	$		$	$
	$	$		$	$
	$	$		$	$
	$	$		$	$
	$	$		$	$
	$	$		$	$
	$	$		$	$
	$	$		$	$
	$	$		$	$
Total	$	$	Total	$	$

Debt Repayment

Creditor	Balance	Paid
	$	$
	$	$
	$	$

Savings

Account	Goal	Amount
	$	$
	$	$

Income

Dates _____

Income Source	Budgeted	Amount	Remaining Income	Amount
	$	$	Total Income	$
	$	$	Total Expenses	$
	$	$	Remaining	$
Total	$	$	Total	$

Expenses

Expense	Budgeted	Amount	Expense	Budgeted	Amount
	$	$		$	$
	$	$		$	$
	$	$		$	$
	$	$		$	$
	$	$		$	$
	$	$		$	$
	$	$		$	$
	$	$		$	$
	$	$		$	$
Total	$	$	Total	$	$

Debt Repayment

Creditor	Balance	Paid
	$	$
	$	$
	$	$

Savings

Account	Goal	Amount
	$	$
	$	$

Income

Dates _____

Income Source	Budgeted	Amount	Remaining Income	Amount
	$	$	Total Income	$
	$	$	Total Expenses	$
	$	$	Remaining	$
Total	$	$	Total	$

Expenses

Expense	Budgeted	Amount	Expense	Budgeted	Amount
	$	$		$	$
	$	$		$	$
	$	$		$	$
	$	$		$	$
	$	$		$	$
	$	$		$	$
	$	$		$	$
	$	$		$	$
	$	$		$	$
Total	$	$	Total	$	$

Debt Repayment

Creditor	Balance	Paid
	$	$
	$	$
	$	$

Savings

Account	Goal	Amount
	$	$
	$	$

Income

Dates _____

Income Source	Budgeted	Amount	Remaining Income	Amount
	$	$	Total Income	$
	$	$	Total Expenses	$
	$	$	Remaining	$
Total	$	$	Total	$

Expenses

Expense	Budgeted	Amount	Expense	Budgeted	Amount
	$	$		$	$
	$	$		$	$
	$	$		$	$
	$	$		$	$
	$	$		$	$
	$	$		$	$
	$	$		$	$
	$	$		$	$
	$	$		$	$
Total	$	$	Total	$	$

Debt Repayment

Creditor	Balance	Paid
	$	$
	$	$
	$	$

Savings

Account	Goal	Amount
	$	$
	$	$

Income

Dates _____

Income Source	Budgeted	Amount	Remaining Income	Amount
	$	$	Total Income	$
	$	$	Total Expenses	$
	$	$	Remaining	$
Total	$	$	Total	$

Expenses

Expense	Budgeted	Amount	Expense	Budgeted	Amount
	$	$		$	$
	$	$		$	$
	$	$		$	$
	$	$		$	$
	$	$		$	$
	$	$		$	$
	$	$		$	$
	$	$		$	$
	$	$		$	$
Total	$	$	Total	$	$

Debt Repayment

Creditor	Balance	Paid
	$	$
	$	$
	$	$

Savings

Account	Goal	Amount
	$	$
	$	$

Income

Dates _____

Income Source	Budgeted	Amount	Remaining Income	Amount
	$	$	Total Income	$
	$	$	Total Expenses	$
	$	$	Remaining	$
Total	$	$	Total	$

Expenses

Expense	Budgeted	Amount	Expense	Budgeted	Amount
	$	$		$	$
	$	$		$	$
	$	$		$	$
	$	$		$	$
	$	$		$	$
	$	$		$	$
	$	$		$	$
	$	$		$	$
	$	$		$	$
Total	$	$	Total	$	$

Debt Repayment

Creditor	Balance	Paid
	$	$
	$	$
	$	$

Savings

Account	Goal	Amount
	$	$
	$	$

Income

Dates _____

Income Source	Budgeted	Amount	Remaining Income	Amount
	$	$	Total Income	$
	$	$	Total Expenses	$
	$	$	Remaining	$
Total	$	$	Total	$

Expenses

Expense	Budgeted	Amount	Expense	Budgeted	Amount
	$	$		$	$
	$	$		$	$
	$	$		$	$
	$	$		$	$
	$	$		$	$
	$	$		$	$
	$	$		$	$
	$	$		$	$
	$	$		$	$
Total	$	$	Total	$	$

Debt Repayment

Creditor	Balance	Paid
	$	$
	$	$
	$	$

Savings

Account	Goal	Amount
	$	$
	$	$

Income

Dates _____

Income Source	Budgeted	Amount	Remaining Income	Amount
	$	$	Total Income	$
	$	$	Total Expenses	$
	$	$	Remaining	$
Total	$	$	Total	$

Expenses

Expense	Budgeted	Amount	Expense	Budgeted	Amount
	$	$		$	$
	$	$		$	$
	$	$		$	$
	$	$		$	$
	$	$		$	$
	$	$		$	$
	$	$		$	$
	$	$		$	$
	$	$		$	$
Total	$	$	Total	$	$

Debt Repayment

Creditor	Balance	Paid
	$	$
	$	$
	$	$

Savings

Account	Goal	Amount
	$	$
	$	$

Income

Dates _____

Income Source	Budgeted	Amount
	$	$
	$	$
	$	$
Total	$	$

Remaining Income	Amount
Total Income	$
Total Expenses	$
Remaining	$
Total	$

Expenses

Expense	Budgeted	Amount
	$	$
	$	$
	$	$
	$	$
	$	$
	$	$
	$	$
	$	$
	$	$
Total	$	$

Expense	Budgeted	Amount
	$	$
	$	$
	$	$
	$	$
	$	$
	$	$
	$	$
	$	$
	$	$
Total	$	$

Debt Repayment

Creditor	Balance	Paid
	$	$
	$	$
	$	$

Savings

Account	Goal	Amount
	$	$
	$	$

Dates _____

Income

Income Source	Budgeted	Amount	Remaining Income	Amount
	$	$	Total Income	$
	$	$	Total Expenses	$
	$	$	Remaining	$
Total	$	$	Total	$

Expenses

Expense	Budgeted	Amount	Expense	Budgeted	Amount
	$	$		$	$
	$	$		$	$
	$	$		$	$
	$	$		$	$
	$	$		$	$
	$	$		$	$
	$	$		$	$
	$	$		$	$
	$	$		$	$
Total	$	$	Total	$	$

Debt Repayment

Creditor	Balance	Paid
	$	$
	$	$
	$	$

Savings

Account	Goal	Amount
	$	$
	$	$

Income

Dates _____

Income Source	Budgeted	Amount	Remaining Income	Amount
	$	$	Total Income	$
	$	$	Total Expenses	$
	$	$	Remaining	$
Total	$	$	Total	$

Expenses

Expense	Budgeted	Amount	Expense	Budgeted	Amount
	$	$		$	$
	$	$		$	$
	$	$		$	$
	$	$		$	$
	$	$		$	$
	$	$		$	$
	$	$		$	$
	$	$		$	$
	$	$		$	$
Total	$	$	Total	$	$

Debt Repayment

Creditor	Balance	Paid
	$	$
	$	$
	$	$

Savings

Account	Goal	Amount
	$	$
	$	$

Income

Dates _____

Income Source	Budgeted	Amount	Remaining Income	Amount
	$	$	Total Income	$
	$	$	Total Expenses	$
	$	$	Remaining	$
Total	$	$	Total	$

Expenses

Expense	Budgeted	Amount	Expense	Budgeted	Amount
	$	$		$	$
	$	$		$	$
	$	$		$	$
	$	$		$	$
	$	$		$	$
	$	$		$	$
	$	$		$	$
	$	$		$	$
	$	$		$	$
Total	$	$	Total	$	$

Debt Repayment

Creditor	Balance	Paid
	$	$
	$	$
	$	$

Savings

Account	Goal	Amount
	$	$
	$	$

Income

Dates _____

Income Source	Budgeted	Amount	Remaining Income	Amount
	$	$	Total Income	$
	$	$	Total Expenses	$
	$	$	Remaining	$
Total	$	$	Total	$

Expenses

Expense	Budgeted	Amount	Expense	Budgeted	Amount
	$	$		$	$
	$	$		$	$
	$	$		$	$
	$	$		$	$
	$	$		$	$
	$	$		$	$
	$	$		$	$
	$	$		$	$
	$	$		$	$
Total	$	$	Total	$	$

Debt Repayment

Creditor	Balance	Paid
	$	$
	$	$
	$	$

Savings

Account	Goal	Amount
	$	$
	$	$

Income

Dates _____

Income Source	Budgeted	Amount	Remaining Income	Amount
	$	$	Total Income	$
	$	$	Total Expenses	$
	$	$	Remaining	$
Total	$	$	Total	$

Expenses

Expense	Budgeted	Amount	Expense	Budgeted	Amount
	$	$		$	$
	$	$		$	$
	$	$		$	$
	$	$		$	$
	$	$		$	$
	$	$		$	$
	$	$		$	$
	$	$		$	$
	$	$		$	$
Total	$	$	Total	$	$

Debt Repayment

Creditor	Balance	Paid
	$	$
	$	$
	$	$

Savings

Account	Goal	Amount
	$	$
	$	$

Income

Dates _____

Income Source	Budgeted	Amount	Remaining Income	Amount
	$	$	Total Income	$
	$	$	Total Expenses	$
	$	$	Remaining	$
Total	$	$	Total	$

Expenses

Expense	Budgeted	Amount	Expense	Budgeted	Amount
	$	$		$	$
	$	$		$	$
	$	$		$	$
	$	$		$	$
	$	$		$	$
	$	$		$	$
	$	$		$	$
	$	$		$	$
	$	$		$	$
Total	$	$	Total	$	$

Debt Repayment

Creditor	Balance	Paid
	$	$
	$	$
	$	$

Savings

Account	Goal	Amount
	$	$
	$	$

Income

Dates _____

Income Source	Budgeted	Amount	Remaining Income	Amount
	$	$	Total Income	$
	$	$	Total Expenses	$
	$	$	Remaining	$
Total	$	$	Total	$

Expenses

Expense	Budgeted	Amount	Expense	Budgeted	Amount
	$	$		$	$
	$	$		$	$
	$	$		$	$
	$	$		$	$
	$	$		$	$
	$	$		$	$
	$	$		$	$
	$	$		$	$
	$	$		$	$
Total	$	$	Total	$	$

Debt Repayment

Creditor	Balance	Paid
	$	$
	$	$
	$	$

Savings

Account	Goal	Amount
	$	$
	$	$

Income

Dates _____

Income Source	Budgeted	Amount	Remaining Income	Amount
	$	$	Total Income	$
	$	$	Total Expenses	$
	$	$	Remaining	$
Total	$	$	Total	$

Expenses

Expense	Budgeted	Amount	Expense	Budgeted	Amount
	$	$		$	$
	$	$		$	$
	$	$		$	$
	$	$		$	$
	$	$		$	$
	$	$		$	$
	$	$		$	$
	$	$		$	$
	$	$		$	$
Total	$	$	Total	$	$

Debt Repayment

Creditor	Balance	Paid
	$	$
	$	$
	$	$

Savings

Account	Goal	Amount
	$	$
	$	$

Income

Dates _____

Income Source	Budgeted	Amount	Remaining Income	Amount
	$	$	Total Income	$
	$	$	Total Expenses	$
	$	$	Remaining	$
Total	$	$	Total	$

Expenses

Expense	Budgeted	Amount	Expense	Budgeted	Amount
	$	$		$	$
	$	$		$	$
	$	$		$	$
	$	$		$	$
	$	$		$	$
	$	$		$	$
	$	$		$	$
	$	$		$	$
	$	$		$	$
Total	$	$	Total	$	$

Debt Repayment

Creditor	Balance	Paid
	$	$
	$	$
	$	$

Savings

Account	Goal	Amount
	$	$
	$	$

Income

Dates _____

Income Source	Budgeted	Amount	Remaining Income	Amount
	$	$	Total Income	$
	$	$	Total Expenses	$
	$	$	Remaining	$
Total	$	$	Total	$

Expenses

Expense	Budgeted	Amount	Expense	Budgeted	Amount
	$	$		$	$
	$	$		$	$
	$	$		$	$
	$	$		$	$
	$	$		$	$
	$	$		$	$
	$	$		$	$
	$	$		$	$
	$	$		$	$
Total	$	$	Total	$	$

Debt Repayment

Creditor	Balance	Paid
	$	$
	$	$
	$	$

Savings

Account	Goal	Amount
	$	$
	$	$

Income

Dates _____

Income Source	Budgeted	Amount	Remaining Income	Amount
	$	$	Total Income	$
	$	$	Total Expenses	$
	$	$	Remaining	$
Total	$	$	Total	$

Expenses

Expense	Budgeted	Amount	Expense	Budgeted	Amount
	$	$		$	$
	$	$		$	$
	$	$		$	$
	$	$		$	$
	$	$		$	$
	$	$		$	$
	$	$		$	$
	$	$		$	$
	$	$		$	$
Total	$	$	Total	$	$

Debt Repayment

Creditor	Balance	Paid
	$	$
	$	$
	$	$

Savings

Account	Goal	Amount
	$	$
	$	$

Income

Dates _____

Income Source	Budgeted	Amount	Remaining Income	Amount
	$	$	Total Income	$
	$	$	Total Expenses	$
	$	$	Remaining	$
Total	$	$	Total	$

Expenses

Expense	Budgeted	Amount	Expense	Budgeted	Amount
	$	$		$	$
	$	$		$	$
	$	$		$	$
	$	$		$	$
	$	$		$	$
	$	$		$	$
	$	$		$	$
	$	$		$	$
	$	$		$	$
Total	$	$	Total	$	$

Debt Repayment

Creditor	Balance	Paid
	$	$
	$	$
	$	$

Savings

Account	Goal	Amount
	$	$
	$	$

Income

Dates _____

Income Source	Budgeted	Amount	Remaining Income	Amount
	$	$	Total Income	$
	$	$	Total Expenses	$
	$	$	Remaining	$
Total	$	$	Total	$

Expenses

Expense	Budgeted	Amount	Expense	Budgeted	Amount
	$	$		$	$
	$	$		$	$
	$	$		$	$
	$	$		$	$
	$	$		$	$
	$	$		$	$
	$	$		$	$
	$	$		$	$
	$	$		$	$
Total	$	$	Total	$	$

Debt Repayment

Creditor	Balance	Paid
	$	$
	$	$
	$	$

Savings

Account	Goal	Amount
	$	$
	$	$

Income

Dates _____

Income Source	Budgeted	Amount	Remaining Income	Amount
	$	$	Total Income	$
	$	$	Total Expenses	$
	$	$	Remaining	$
Total	$	$	Total	$

Expenses

Expense	Budgeted	Amount	Expense	Budgeted	Amount
	$	$		$	$
	$	$		$	$
	$	$		$	$
	$	$		$	$
	$	$		$	$
	$	$		$	$
	$	$		$	$
	$	$		$	$
	$	$		$	$
Total	$	$	Total	$	$

Debt Repayment

Creditor	Balance	Paid
	$	$
	$	$
	$	$

Savings

Account	Goal	Amount
	$	$
	$	$

Income

Dates _____

Income Source	Budgeted	Amount	Remaining Income	Amount
	$	$	Total Income	$
	$	$	Total Expenses	$
	$	$	Remaining	$
Total	$	$	Total	$

Expenses

Expense	Budgeted	Amount	Expense	Budgeted	Amount
	$	$		$	$
	$	$		$	$
	$	$		$	$
	$	$		$	$
	$	$		$	$
	$	$		$	$
	$	$		$	$
	$	$		$	$
	$	$		$	$
Total	$	$	Total	$	$

Debt Repayment

Creditor	Balance	Paid
	$	$
	$	$
	$	$

Savings

Account	Goal	Amount
	$	$
	$	$

Income

Dates _____

Income Source	Budgeted	Amount	Remaining Income	Amount
	$	$	Total Income	$
	$	$	Total Expenses	$
	$	$	Remaining	$
Total	$	$	Total	$

Expenses

Expense	Budgeted	Amount	Expense	Budgeted	Amount
	$	$		$	$
	$	$		$	$
	$	$		$	$
	$	$		$	$
	$	$		$	$
	$	$		$	$
	$	$		$	$
	$	$		$	$
	$	$		$	$
Total	$	$	Total	$	$

Debt Repayment

Creditor	Balance	Paid
	$	$
	$	$
	$	$

Savings

Account	Goal	Amount
	$	$
	$	$

Income

Dates _____

Income Source	Budgeted	Amount	Remaining Income	Amount
	$	$	Total Income	$
	$	$	Total Expenses	$
	$	$	Remaining	$
Total	$	$	Total	$

Expenses

Expense	Budgeted	Amount	Expense	Budgeted	Amount
	$	$		$	$
	$	$		$	$
	$	$		$	$
	$	$		$	$
	$	$		$	$
	$	$		$	$
	$	$		$	$
	$	$		$	$
	$	$		$	$
Total	$	$	Total	$	$

Debt Repayment

Creditor	Balance	Paid
	$	$
	$	$
	$	$

Savings

Account	Goal	Amount
	$	$
	$	$

Income

Dates _____

Income Source	Budgeted	Amount	Remaining Income	Amount
	$	$	Total Income	$
	$	$	Total Expenses	$
	$	$	Remaining	$
Total	$	$	Total	$

Expenses

Expense	Budgeted	Amount	Expense	Budgeted	Amount
	$	$		$	$
	$	$		$	$
	$	$		$	$
	$	$		$	$
	$	$		$	$
	$	$		$	$
	$	$		$	$
	$	$		$	$
	$	$		$	$
Total	$	$	Total	$	$

Debt Repayment

Creditor	Balance	Paid
	$	$
	$	$
	$	$

Savings

Account	Goal	Amount
	$	$
	$	$

Income

Dates _____

Income Source	Budgeted	Amount	Remaining Income	Amount
	$	$	Total Income	$
	$	$	Total Expenses	$
	$	$	Remaining	$
Total	$	$	Total	$

Expenses

Expense	Budgeted	Amount	Expense	Budgeted	Amount
	$	$		$	$
	$	$		$	$
	$	$		$	$
	$	$		$	$
	$	$		$	$
	$	$		$	$
	$	$		$	$
	$	$		$	$
	$	$		$	$
Total	$	$	Total	$	$

Debt Repayment

Creditor	Balance	Paid
	$	$
	$	$
	$	$

Savings

Account	Goal	Amount
	$	$
	$	$

Income

Dates _____

Income Source	Budgeted	Amount	Remaining Income	Amount
	$	$	Total Income	$
	$	$	Total Expenses	$
	$	$	Remaining	$
Total	$	$	Total	$

Expenses

Expense	Budgeted	Amount	Expense	Budgeted	Amount
	$	$		$	$
	$	$		$	$
	$	$		$	$
	$	$		$	$
	$	$		$	$
	$	$		$	$
	$	$		$	$
	$	$		$	$
	$	$		$	$
Total	$	$	Total	$	$

Debt Repayment

Creditor	Balance	Paid
	$	$
	$	$
	$	$

Savings

Account	Goal	Amount
	$	$
	$	$

Dates _____

Income

Income Source	Budgeted	Amount	Remaining Income	Amount
	$	$	Total Income	$
	$	$	Total Expenses	$
	$	$	Remaining	$
Total	$	$	Total	$

Expenses

Expense	Budgeted	Amount	Expense	Budgeted	Amount
	$	$		$	$
	$	$		$	$
	$	$		$	$
	$	$		$	$
	$	$		$	$
	$	$		$	$
	$	$		$	$
	$	$		$	$
	$	$		$	$
Total	$	$	Total	$	$

Debt Repayment

Creditor	Balance	Paid
	$	$
	$	$
	$	$

Savings

Account	Goal	Amount
	$	$
	$	$

Income

Dates _____

Income Source	Budgeted	Amount	Remaining Income	Amount
	$	$	Total Income	$
	$	$	Total Expenses	$
	$	$	Remaining	$
Total	$	$	Total	$

Expenses

Expense	Budgeted	Amount	Expense	Budgeted	Amount
	$	$		$	$
	$	$		$	$
	$	$		$	$
	$	$		$	$
	$	$		$	$
	$	$		$	$
	$	$		$	$
	$	$		$	$
	$	$		$	$
Total	$	$	Total	$	$

Debt Repayment

Creditor	Balance	Paid
	$	$
	$	$
	$	$

Savings

Account	Goal	Amount
	$	$
	$	$

Income

Dates _____

Income Source	Budgeted	Amount	Remaining Income	Amount
	$	$	Total Income	$
	$	$	Total Expenses	$
	$	$	Remaining	$
Total	$	$	Total	$

Expenses

Expense	Budgeted	Amount	Expense	Budgeted	Amount
	$	$		$	$
	$	$		$	$
	$	$		$	$
	$	$		$	$
	$	$		$	$
	$	$		$	$
	$	$		$	$
	$	$		$	$
	$	$		$	$
Total	$	$	Total	$	$

Debt Repayment

Creditor	Balance	Paid
	$	$
	$	$
	$	$

Savings

Account	Goal	Amount
	$	$
	$	$

Income

Dates _____

Income Source	Budgeted	Amount	Remaining Income	Amount
	$	$	Total Income	$
	$	$	Total Expenses	$
	$	$	Remaining	$
Total	$	$	Total	$

Expenses

Expense	Budgeted	Amount	Expense	Budgeted	Amount
	$	$		$	$
	$	$		$	$
	$	$		$	$
	$	$		$	$
	$	$		$	$
	$	$		$	$
	$	$		$	$
	$	$		$	$
	$	$		$	$
Total	$	$	Total	$	$

Debt Repayment

Creditor	Balance	Paid
	$	$
	$	$
	$	$

Savings

Account	Goal	Amount
	$	$
	$	$

Income

Dates _____

Income Source	Budgeted	Amount	Remaining Income	Amount
	$	$	Total Income	$
	$	$	Total Expenses	$
	$	$	Remaining	$
Total	$	$	Total	$

Expenses

Expense	Budgeted	Amount	Expense	Budgeted	Amount
	$	$		$	$
	$	$		$	$
	$	$		$	$
	$	$		$	$
	$	$		$	$
	$	$		$	$
	$	$		$	$
	$	$		$	$
	$	$		$	$
Total	$	$	Total	$	$

Debt Repayment

Creditor	Balance	Paid
	$	$
	$	$
	$	$

Savings

Account	Goal	Amount
	$	$
	$	$

Income

Dates _____

Income Source	Budgeted	Amount	Remaining Income	Amount
	$	$	Total Income	$
	$	$	Total Expenses	$
	$	$	Remaining	$
Total	$	$	Total	$

Expenses

Expense	Budgeted	Amount	Expense	Budgeted	Amount
	$	$		$	$
	$	$		$	$
	$	$		$	$
	$	$		$	$
	$	$		$	$
	$	$		$	$
	$	$		$	$
	$	$		$	$
	$	$		$	$
Total	$	$	Total	$	$

Debt Repayment

Creditor	Balance	Paid
	$	$
	$	$
	$	$

Savings

Account	Goal	Amount
	$	$
	$	$

Income

Dates _____

Income Source	Budgeted	Amount	Remaining Income	Amount
	$	$	Total Income	$
	$	$	Total Expenses	$
	$	$	Remaining	$
Total	$	$	Total	$

Expenses

Expense	Budgeted	Amount	Expense	Budgeted	Amount
	$	$		$	$
	$	$		$	$
	$	$		$	$
	$	$		$	$
	$	$		$	$
	$	$		$	$
	$	$		$	$
	$	$		$	$
	$	$		$	$
Total	$	$	Total	$	$

Debt Repayment

Creditor	Balance	Paid
	$	$
	$	$
	$	$

Savings

Account	Goal	Amount
	$	$
	$	$

Income

Dates _____

Income Source	Budgeted	Amount	Remaining Income	Amount
	$	$	Total Income	$
	$	$	Total Expenses	$
	$	$	Remaining	$
Total	$	$	Total	$

Expenses

Expense	Budgeted	Amount	Expense	Budgeted	Amount
	$	$		$	$
	$	$		$	$
	$	$		$	$
	$	$		$	$
	$	$		$	$
	$	$		$	$
	$	$		$	$
	$	$		$	$
	$	$		$	$
Total	$	$	Total	$	$

Debt Repayment

Creditor	Balance	Paid
	$	$
	$	$
	$	$

Savings

Account	Goal	Amount
	$	$
	$	$

Income

Dates _____

Income Source	Budgeted	Amount	Remaining Income	Amount
	$	$	Total Income	$
	$	$	Total Expenses	$
	$	$	Remaining	$
Total	$	$	Total	$

Expenses

Expense	Budgeted	Amount	Expense	Budgeted	Amount
	$	$		$	$
	$	$		$	$
	$	$		$	$
	$	$		$	$
	$	$		$	$
	$	$		$	$
	$	$		$	$
	$	$		$	$
	$	$		$	$
Total	$	$	Total	$	$

Debt Repayment

Creditor	Balance	Paid
	$	$
	$	$
	$	$

Savings

Account	Goal	Amount
	$	$
	$	$

Income

Dates _____

Income Source	Budgeted	Amount	Remaining Income	Amount
	$	$	Total Income	$
	$	$	Total Expenses	$
	$	$	Remaining	$
Total	$	$	Total	$

Expenses

Expense	Budgeted	Amount	Expense	Budgeted	Amount
	$	$		$	$
	$	$		$	$
	$	$		$	$
	$	$		$	$
	$	$		$	$
	$	$		$	$
	$	$		$	$
	$	$		$	$
	$	$		$	$
Total	$	$	Total	$	$

Debt Repayment

Creditor	Balance	Paid
	$	$
	$	$
	$	$

Savings

Account	Goal	Amount
	$	$
	$	$

Income

Dates _____

Income Source	Budgeted	Amount	Remaining Income	Amount
	$	$	Total Income	$
	$	$	Total Expenses	$
	$	$	Remaining	$
Total	$	$	Total	$

Expenses

Expense	Budgeted	Amount	Expense	Budgeted	Amount
	$	$		$	$
	$	$		$	$
	$	$		$	$
	$	$		$	$
	$	$		$	$
	$	$		$	$
	$	$		$	$
	$	$		$	$
	$	$		$	$
Total	$	$	Total	$	$

Debt Repayment

Creditor	Balance	Paid
	$	$
	$	$
	$	$

Savings

Account	Goal	Amount
	$	$
	$	$

Income

Dates _____

Income Source	Budgeted	Amount	Remaining Income	Amount
	$	$	Total Income	$
	$	$	Total Expenses	$
	$	$	Remaining	$
Total	$	$	Total	$

Expenses

Expense	Budgeted	Amount	Expense	Budgeted	Amount
	$	$		$	$
	$	$		$	$
	$	$		$	$
	$	$		$	$
	$	$		$	$
	$	$		$	$
	$	$		$	$
	$	$		$	$
	$	$		$	$
Total	$	$	Total	$	$

Debt Repayment

Creditor		Balance	Paid
		$	$
		$	$
		$	$

Savings

Account		Goal	Amount
		$	$
		$	$

Dates _____

Income

Income Source	Budgeted	Amount	Remaining Income	Amount
	$	$	Total Income	$
	$	$	Total Expenses	$
	$	$	Remaining	$
Total	$	$	Total	$

Expenses

Expense	Budgeted	Amount	Expense	Budgeted	Amount
	$	$		$	$
	$	$		$	$
	$	$		$	$
	$	$		$	$
	$	$		$	$
	$	$		$	$
	$	$		$	$
	$	$		$	$
	$	$		$	$
Total	$	$	Total	$	$

Debt Repayment

Creditor	Balance	Paid
	$	$
	$	$
	$	$

Savings

Account	Goal	Amount
	$	$
	$	$

Income

Dates _____

Income Source	Budgeted	Amount	Remaining Income	Amount
	$	$	Total Income	$
	$	$	Total Expenses	$
	$	$	Remaining	$
Total	$	$	Total	$

Expenses

Expense	Budgeted	Amount	Expense	Budgeted	Amount
	$	$		$	$
	$	$		$	$
	$	$		$	$
	$	$		$	$
	$	$		$	$
	$	$		$	$
	$	$		$	$
	$	$		$	$
	$	$		$	$
Total	$	$	Total	$	$

Debt Repayment

Creditor	Balance	Paid
	$	$
	$	$
	$	$

Savings

Account	Goal	Amount
	$	$
	$	$

Income

Dates _____

Income Source	Budgeted	Amount	Remaining Income	Amount
	$	$	Total Income	$
	$	$	Total Expenses	$
	$	$	Remaining	$
Total	$	$	Total	$

Expenses

Expense	Budgeted	Amount	Expense	Budgeted	Amount
	$	$		$	$
	$	$		$	$
	$	$		$	$
	$	$		$	$
	$	$		$	$
	$	$		$	$
	$	$		$	$
	$	$		$	$
	$	$		$	$
Total	$	$	Total	$	$

Debt Repayment

Creditor	Balance	Paid
	$	$
	$	$
	$	$

Savings

Account	Goal	Amount
	$	$
	$	$

Income

Dates _____

Income Source	Budgeted	Amount	Remaining Income	Amount
	$	$	Total Income	$
	$	$	Total Expenses	$
	$	$	Remaining	$
Total	$	$	Total	$

Expenses

Expense	Budgeted	Amount	Expense	Budgeted	Amount
	$	$		$	$
	$	$		$	$
	$	$		$	$
	$	$		$	$
	$	$		$	$
	$	$		$	$
	$	$		$	$
	$	$		$	$
	$	$		$	$
Total	$	$	Total	$	$

Debt Repayment

Creditor	Balance	Paid
	$	$
	$	$
	$	$

Savings

Account	Goal	Amount
	$	$
	$	$

Income

Dates _____

Income Source	Budgeted	Amount	Remaining Income	Amount
	$	$	Total Income	$
	$	$	Total Expenses	$
	$	$	Remaining	$
Total	$	$	Total	$

Expenses

Expense	Budgeted	Amount	Expense	Budgeted	Amount
	$	$		$	$
	$	$		$	$
	$	$		$	$
	$	$		$	$
	$	$		$	$
	$	$		$	$
	$	$		$	$
	$	$		$	$
	$	$		$	$
Total	$	$	Total	$	$

Debt Repayment

Creditor	Balance	Paid
	$	$
	$	$
	$	$

Savings

Account	Goal	Amount
	$	$
	$	$

Income

Dates _____

Income Source	Budgeted	Amount	Remaining Income	Amount
	$	$	Total Income	$
	$	$	Total Expenses	$
	$	$	Remaining	$
Total	$	$	Total	$

Expenses

Expense	Budgeted	Amount	Expense	Budgeted	Amount
	$	$		$	$
	$	$		$	$
	$	$		$	$
	$	$		$	$
	$	$		$	$
	$	$		$	$
	$	$		$	$
	$	$		$	$
	$	$		$	$
Total	$	$	Total	$	$

Debt Repayment

Creditor	Balance	Paid
	$	$
	$	$
	$	$

Savings

Account	Goal	Amount
	$	$
	$	$

Income

Dates _____

Income Source	Budgeted	Amount	Remaining Income	Amount
	$	$	Total Income	$
	$	$	Total Expenses	$
	$	$	Remaining	$
Total	$	$	Total	$

Expenses

Expense	Budgeted	Amount	Expense	Budgeted	Amount
	$	$		$	$
	$	$		$	$
	$	$		$	$
	$	$		$	$
	$	$		$	$
	$	$		$	$
	$	$		$	$
	$	$		$	$
	$	$		$	$
Total	$	$	Total	$	$

Debt Repayment

Creditor	Balance	Paid
	$	$
	$	$
	$	$

Savings

Account	Goal	Amount
	$	$
	$	$

Income

Dates _____

Income Source	Budgeted	Amount	Remaining Income	Amount
	$	$	Total Income	$
	$	$	Total Expenses	$
	$	$	Remaining	$
Total	$	$	Total	$

Expenses

Expense	Budgeted	Amount	Expense	Budgeted	Amount
	$	$		$	$
	$	$		$	$
	$	$		$	$
	$	$		$	$
	$	$		$	$
	$	$		$	$
	$	$		$	$
	$	$		$	$
	$	$		$	$
Total	$	$	Total	$	$

Debt Repayment

Creditor	Balance	Paid
	$	$
	$	$
	$	$

Savings

Account	Goal	Amount
	$	$
	$	$

Income

Dates _____

Income Source	Budgeted	Amount	Remaining Income	Amount
	$	$	Total Income	$
	$	$	Total Expenses	$
	$	$	Remaining	$
Total	$	$	Total	$

Expenses

Expense	Budgeted	Amount	Expense	Budgeted	Amount
	$	$		$	$
	$	$		$	$
	$	$		$	$
	$	$		$	$
	$	$		$	$
	$	$		$	$
	$	$		$	$
	$	$		$	$
	$	$		$	$
Total	$	$	Total	$	$

Debt Repayment

Creditor	Balance	Paid
	$	$
	$	$
	$	$

Savings

Account	Goal	Amount
	$	$
	$	$

Income

Dates _____

Income Source	Budgeted	Amount	Remaining Income	Amount
	$	$	Total Income	$
	$	$	Total Expenses	$
	$	$	Remaining	$
Total	$	$	Total	$

Expenses

Expense	Budgeted	Amount	Expense	Budgeted	Amount
	$	$		$	$
	$	$		$	$
	$	$		$	$
	$	$		$	$
	$	$		$	$
	$	$		$	$
	$	$		$	$
	$	$		$	$
	$	$		$	$
Total	$	$	Total	$	$

Debt Repayment

Creditor	Balance	Paid
	$	$
	$	$
	$	$

Savings

Account	Goal	Amount
	$	$
	$	$

Income

Dates _____

Income Source	Budgeted	Amount	Remaining Income	Amount
	$	$	Total Income	$
	$	$	Total Expenses	$
	$	$	Remaining	$
Total	$	$	Total	$

Expenses

Expense	Budgeted	Amount	Expense	Budgeted	Amount
	$	$		$	$
	$	$		$	$
	$	$		$	$
	$	$		$	$
	$	$		$	$
	$	$		$	$
	$	$		$	$
	$	$		$	$
	$	$		$	$
Total	$	$	Total	$	$

Debt Repayment

Creditor	Balance	Paid
	$	$
	$	$
	$	$

Savings

Account	Goal	Amount
	$	$
	$	$

Income

Dates _____

Income Source	Budgeted	Amount	Remaining Income	Amount
	$	$	Total Income	$
	$	$	Total Expenses	$
	$	$	Remaining	$
Total	$	$	Total	$

Expenses

Expense	Budgeted	Amount	Expense	Budgeted	Amount
	$	$		$	$
	$	$		$	$
	$	$		$	$
	$	$		$	$
	$	$		$	$
	$	$		$	$
	$	$		$	$
	$	$		$	$
	$	$		$	$
Total	$	$	Total	$	$

Debt Repayment

Creditor	Balance	Paid
	$	$
	$	$
	$	$

Savings

Account	Goal	Amount
	$	$
	$	$

Income

Dates _____

Income Source	Budgeted	Amount	Remaining Income	Amount
	$	$	Total Income	$
	$	$	Total Expenses	$
	$	$	Remaining	$
Total	$	$	Total	$

Expenses

Expense	Budgeted	Amount	Expense	Budgeted	Amount
	$	$		$	$
	$	$		$	$
	$	$		$	$
	$	$		$	$
	$	$		$	$
	$	$		$	$
	$	$		$	$
	$	$		$	$
	$	$		$	$
Total	$	$	Total	$	$

Debt Repayment

Creditor	Balance	Paid
	$	$
	$	$
	$	$

Savings

Account	Goal	Amount
	$	$
	$	$

Income

Dates _____

Income Source	Budgeted	Amount	Remaining Income	Amount
	$	$	Total Income	$
	$	$	Total Expenses	$
	$	$	Remaining	$
Total	$	$	Total	$

Expenses

Expense	Budgeted	Amount	Expense	Budgeted	Amount
	$	$		$	$
	$	$		$	$
	$	$		$	$
	$	$		$	$
	$	$		$	$
	$	$		$	$
	$	$		$	$
	$	$		$	$
	$	$		$	$
Total	$	$	Total	$	$

Debt Repayment

Creditor	Balance	Paid
	$	$
	$	$
	$	$

Savings

Account	Goal	Amount
	$	$
	$	$

Income

Dates _____

Income Source	Budgeted	Amount	Remaining Income	Amount
	$	$	Total Income	$
	$	$	Total Expenses	$
	$	$	Remaining	$
Total	$	$	Total	$

Expenses

Expense	Budgeted	Amount	Expense	Budgeted	Amount
	$	$		$	$
	$	$		$	$
	$	$		$	$
	$	$		$	$
	$	$		$	$
	$	$		$	$
	$	$		$	$
	$	$		$	$
	$	$		$	$
Total	$	$	Total	$	$

Debt Repayment

Creditor	Balance	Paid
	$	$
	$	$
	$	$

Savings

Account	Goal	Amount
	$	$
	$	$

Income

Dates _____

Income Source	Budgeted	Amount	Remaining Income	Amount
	$	$	Total Income	$
	$	$	Total Expenses	$
	$	$	Remaining	$
Total	$	$	Total	$

Expenses

Expense	Budgeted	Amount	Expense	Budgeted	Amount
	$	$		$	$
	$	$		$	$
	$	$		$	$
	$	$		$	$
	$	$		$	$
	$	$		$	$
	$	$		$	$
	$	$		$	$
	$	$		$	$
Total	$	$	Total	$	$

Debt Repayment

Creditor	Balance	Paid
	$	$
	$	$
	$	$

Savings

Account	Goal	Amount
	$	$
	$	$

Income

Dates _____

Income Source	Budgeted	Amount	Remaining Income	Amount
	$	$	Total Income	$
	$	$	Total Expenses	$
	$	$	Remaining	$
Total	$	$	Total	$

Expenses

Expense	Budgeted	Amount	Expense	Budgeted	Amount
	$	$		$	$
	$	$		$	$
	$	$		$	$
	$	$		$	$
	$	$		$	$
	$	$		$	$
	$	$		$	$
	$	$		$	$
	$	$		$	$
Total	$	$	Total	$	$

Debt Repayment

Creditor	Balance	Paid
	$	$
	$	$
	$	$

Savings

Account	Goal	Amount
	$	$
	$	$

Income

Dates _____

Income Source	Budgeted	Amount	Remaining Income	Amount
	$	$	Total Income	$
	$	$	Total Expenses	$
	$	$	Remaining	$
Total	$	$	Total	$

Expenses

Expense	Budgeted	Amount	Expense	Budgeted	Amount
	$	$		$	$
	$	$		$	$
	$	$		$	$
	$	$		$	$
	$	$		$	$
	$	$		$	$
	$	$		$	$
	$	$		$	$
	$	$		$	$
Total	$	$	Total	$	$

Debt Repayment

Creditor	Balance	Paid
	$	$
	$	$
	$	$

Savings

Account	Goal	Amount
	$	$
	$	$

Income

Dates _____

Income Source	Budgeted	Amount	Remaining Income	Amount
	$	$	Total Income	$
	$	$	Total Expenses	$
	$	$	Remaining	$
Total	$	$	Total	$

Expenses

Expense	Budgeted	Amount	Expense	Budgeted	Amount
	$	$		$	$
	$	$		$	$
	$	$		$	$
	$	$		$	$
	$	$		$	$
	$	$		$	$
	$	$		$	$
	$	$		$	$
	$	$		$	$
Total	$	$	Total	$	$

Debt Repayment

Creditor	Balance	Paid
	$	$
	$	$
	$	$

Savings

Account	Goal	Amount
	$	$
	$	$

Income

Dates _____

Income Source	Budgeted	Amount	Remaining Income	Amount
	$	$	Total Income	$
	$	$	Total Expenses	$
	$	$	Remaining	$
Total	$	$	Total	$

Expenses

Expense	Budgeted	Amount	Expense	Budgeted	Amount
	$	$		$	$
	$	$		$	$
	$	$		$	$
	$	$		$	$
	$	$		$	$
	$	$		$	$
	$	$		$	$
	$	$		$	$
	$	$		$	$
Total	$	$	Total	$	$

Debt Repayment

Creditor		Balance	Paid
		$	$
		$	$
		$	$

Savings

Account		Goal	Amount
		$	$
		$	$

www.ingramcontent.com/pod-product-compliance
Lightning Source LLC
Chambersburg PA
CBHW081428220526
45466CB00008B/2299